Believe

FIVE STEPS TO FREEDOM

Believe

FIVE STEPS TO FREEDOM

JASON B. ORR

This book is protected by copyright laws of the United States of America. This book may not be copied or reprinted for commercial gain or profit. The use of short quotations or occasional page copying for personal or group study is permitted and encouraged. Permission will be granted upon request.

Scripture taken from the New King James Version®. Copyright © 1982 by Thomas Nelson. Used by permission. All rights reserved.

Scripture quotations marked (NIV) are taken from the Holy Bible, New International Version®, NIV®. Copyright © 1973, 1978, 1984, 2011 by Biblica, Inc.™ Used by permission of Zondervan. All rights reserved worldwide. www.zondervan.com The "NIV" and "New International Version" are trademarks registered in the United States Patent and Trademark Office by Biblica, Inc.™

Scripture quotations marked (NLT) are taken from the Holy Bible, New Living Translation, copyright © 1996, 2004, 2015 by Tyndale House Foundation. Used by permission of Tyndale House Publishers, Carol Stream, Illinois 60188. All rights reserved.

GOD MANIFEST PUBLISHING
www.GodManifestPublishing.com

This book and all other God Manifest Publishing and God Manifest Publishing Fiction books are available on Amazon.com.

Cover and interior designed by Jonnathan Zin Truong
For more information on foreign distributors, email publishers@godmanifestpublishing.com
Reach us at on the internet: www.GodManifestPublishing.com

ISBN: 978-1-7340556-3-4
eBook: ISBN: 978-1-7340556-4-1

Printed in the United States of America.
Copyright © 2021 Jason B. Orr
All rights reserved.

DEDICATION

To my wife:
Your undying faith and dedication to God has been an inspiration to me. Your innocence and joy brought life, and light, into the darkness I was trapped in. You are my anchor. Because of you, I found my faith, my purpose, and my identity.

To my three sons:
I pray every day that you find identity and purpose in God. That He leads and guides you the way He has me, and that you all become better men, husbands, and fathers than I ever was or dreamed was possible.

To my dad:
You mean more to me than words could ever tell. My life would be very different if you had not chosen me to carry your name. I am who I have become in no small part because you were there. I am proud of you and your service to our country.

To my mother:
We would not be who we are today without the choices you made. Your desire to know and do God's will is what made us who we are. Your prayers and devotion to your faith opened doors and saved lives, including mine. You are my hero.

TABLE OF CONTENTS

Foreword 9
Prayer 13
Preface 15
Chapter 1: My Journey 17
    Fear 17
    But God! 20
    Letting Go 21
Chapter 2: Believe 23
    Grandmother 26
    The Fight 29
    No God 36
    The One 38
    The Process 42
Chapter 3: Faith 45
    The Secret 45
    Seek and You Will Find 47
    Trial By Fire 55
    Answers 60
    Evidence 63
    Faith Simplified 65
Chapter 4: Loving God 69
    Communication 70
    Trust 74
    Submit 77
    Born Again 79
    Purpose 81

Chapter 5: Loving You 89
    Storms 90
    The Mirror 93
    Next 104
    Freedom 108

Chapter 6: Loving Them 113
    Change 115
    Hope 117
    New Life 120
    Unconditional Love 123

Chapter 7: Conclusion 127
    Unity of Belief 127
    Foundations of Faith 130
    Love God 131
    Love the New You 132
    Love Others 134
    The Call 136

FOREWORD

Can you imagine yourself living in a totally isolated setting and the only reading material available to you is a Bible? What would your personal theology look like?

We might begin our quest for knowledge with the question, "What is truth?" Are we left with the answer to that question, or do we stand in jest like Pilate did without an answer?

Academically, we know that truth is both concrete and absolute. Today, we often consider truth to be an interpretation of the truth that, at times, evolves to fit a narrative at that point in time. Don't our responses to deep questions often begin with, "Well, I feel that …"? What is the truth?

A few years back, Jason Orr and I crossed paths while attending the same church. Jason invited me to attend a Bible study and I accepted that invitation. After some discussion, Jason explained that his vision of a study would entail just him and myself setting out on a word study and seeing where God led us. My initial thoughts were that a small group of men would sit in a circle, discuss certain Scriptures, and analyze said Scriptures like a think tank. Jason's explanation pushed me a bit out of my comfort zone, and I knew that time would need to be invested and time was a commodity that I was short on. But nonetheless, we began an intentional deep dive, and our study took us in directions that neither of us had expected. From Jason's seminary studies, we employed tools that helped us focus on one specific word, "trust," and we relentlessly pursued that word throughout the testaments. We considered the historical context, the original language, and how it cross-referenced with other passages where it was mentioned. Over time, others joined in and we truly witnessed how iron sharpens iron. Who knew where this would all lead when we simply said yes to what God had called us both to do?

A few years had passed when I invited Jason to attend a men's Christian retreat for veterans and first responders to help serve on a prayer team. Jason was obviously out of his comfort zone (touché) but accepted the invitation with some reservation.

Today, I am grateful that Jason and I both serve as leaders in that same church, C3 Victory in Victoria, Texas. And I am grateful that together we both serve the men and women at Christian Warriors Retreat. Our friendship, brotherhood, and obedience to stepping out of our comfort zones have led us to witness miracle after miracle. Who knew, other than God, where this all would lead, and will still lead? I can say that there are far fewer reservations these days when God calls either of us into uncharted territories.

Jason does not intend for you to take his word on what truth is, but rather he hopes that you will take it upon yourself to seek out the truth, grasp it, and incorporate it into your personal theology. Then, take the truth that is revealed to you and share it with others. This is how we make disciples and set the captives free. Only the truth can do that. But first things first, know the truth for yourself, and the truth will set you free.

Dan Pooley
Elder, C3 Victory in Victoria, Texas

MARK 9:23 (NKJV)

Jesus said to him, *"If you can believe, all things are possible to him who believes."*

PRAYER

God, bless this book and all who read it. May your words reach those who mine would not. May your love be made manifest in their hearts, and may their words and works become yours. May they find redemption in your Holy Spirit and your faith be made the foundation of their lives. Let them move forward on the path you have called them to, and may their bodies, minds, and homes be healed.

Thank you, Father, for leading me, breaking me, and molding me. Thank you for protecting me and making me more like you. Thank you, Father, for doing the same with each and every reader of this book.

In Jesus's name, I pray. Amen!

PREFACE

There have only been a handful of people whom I have allowed to influence my life. These people were often unaware that their actions, and words, had such sway. I have come to realize that, in this same way, there are people in my life who, either in passing or in relationship, have allowed me to be an influence in their lives. This realization was, and continues to be, an enormous responsibility and honor, one that I do not take lightly.

I had a rough childhood, to say the least, and relationships were not an easy thing. My home life was precarious at best, but mostly just scary. We had no money most of the time, and so the housing we lived in was almost always less than desirable. Most of the time my clothes came from other people, but only after they had thoroughly worn them. When it comes to shoes, I can honestly say that I have walked a mile in those belonging to another man.

The almost-daily physical abuse and the ever-more-frequent verbal and emotional abuse created an environment that was tenuous at best. Though I have had several stepdads, this particular one was not happy, and he made sure that no one else was either. As an adult, I bear no ill feelings toward this man. In fact, I pray that his life has found peace. I pray that blessing and favor follow him and that happiness fills his home.

The past is the past. The result of mine, however, was a boy broken. I had a case of PTSD so bad that even into my late twenties and early thirties, I was unable to function effectively in social environments. If someone were to make any sudden movements, I would flinch. If anyone got angry, the urge to flee was almost overwhelming. More than a decade of hate and hurt had created a weak, frail, and sad man. A man with very little self-confidence and even less motivation. My fear was bottled up nice and tight, until I was stressed, backed into a corner, and pushed to anger. When that happened, things would get broken. I was so scared that the only time I could relieve my stress and frustration was on the people I cared about. Only then was I comfortable enough to let go of my anger. I was so scared I couldn't even be angry at the right people. You can imagine then how very blessed I was to find a woman who could see the man I could be and not the man I was. I have called that woman "wife" and "best friend" for twenty-three years.

It is my prayer that this book provides you with insights that will allow you to find yourself in God. That your identity and purpose would be revealed. That if you apply these principles, you will be able to find healing in body, mind, and soul that will allow you to become the light that someone you may know, or haven't yet met, needs. That once that light turns on, it can never be put out, even in death. May all those who read this find freedom.

Please note that the stories from my life are not all told in chronological order. A few are told in a particular context to emphasize an idea, but all are true depictions of those times in my life. My hope is that the weakness in my life can bring strength into yours.

Chapter 1
MY JOURNEY

Fear

My friend Scott had known me when I was a young boy. We had lost touch over the years, but eventually found ourselves going to the same church. He and I had taken our families to Garner State Park one summer and were in the middle of one of the best camping trips I had ever been on. Scott is like the ultimate Boy Scout. He can build just about anything, he cooks, he is a certified diver, and when we went camping, let's just say I found myself actually looking for the kitchen sink and I found it too. We had elk steaks, hamburgers, eggs, bacon, and coffee with a percolator. He brought a stove top and several coolers with meats and drinks, including milk. He brought tables, chairs, an actual camping sink, potable water, and an empty container to catch the used water in. He had tents, firewood, charcoal, matches, diving gear, two kayaks (with their paddles), an axe, knives, forks, spoons, bowls, and other dishes including frying pans and a few pots, and a partridge in a pear tree. This is the second and last time my wife and I ever went camping in twenty-three years. He ruined her. Now if we wanted to go camping, but I could not bring all of these things, she refuses to participate (unless it is a trip to a hotel).

But on this particular trip, we were cooking dinner at our campsite (the envy of all of the surrounding campers, by the way), and my twins, who were eight at the time, were acting up. They were knocking things over and running around, kids being kids. I, however, did not see it that way at the time. I admittedly was a bit gruff with them, but I was able to get them to calm down. However, Scott saw it differently. From the outside, Scott saw a man telling kids not to be kids. A spirit-breaking moment I had been through as a kid and purposefully had been trying to forget. Here I was doing the exact same thing and oblivious to that fact. Scott pulled me to the side and asked me why I felt the need to talk to my kids in that way. I explained to him that I needed them to behave, and I felt it inappropriate for them to be running around like heathens breaking things that did not belong to them. Scott had packed an answer for that too.

After intently listening to everything I had to say, Scott proceeded to ask one profound question, "What are you afraid of?" His question caught me off guard. After knowing me for as long as he had, how could he think I was afraid of anything?

Scott, being Scott, simply said, "Next time you feel yourself getting angry, ask yourself that question." I belligerently stated that I was not afraid of anything and that I failed to see how that had anything to do with what my kids were doing. He insisted that I at least try it, and so to make this awkward situation pass, I agreed. I told him that "next time" I would try. The miracle of this entire encounter was that I actually did try it.

> Wounds from a friend can be trusted,
> but an enemy multiplies kisses.
> **Proverbs 27:6 (NIV)**

It was a few weeks later when my kids, again being kids, were on my last nerve. I began to feel myself getting angry, and I instantly remembered Scott's words at the campsite. At that moment, I thought, "Why not?" After all, what did I have to lose? I began to ask myself what I was afraid of. What was it that they were doing that was causing me to possibly be afraid? And of what?

Chapter 1: My Journey

Almost immediately, the answers, although unwelcome, began flooding my thoughts. I was afraid that one of the kids may get hurt and it would be my fault because I didn't make them stop. I was afraid that others would think poorly of me because they got hurt. I was afraid that my neighbors would hear them yelling and carrying on and be upset because we were disturbing them. I was afraid that they were going to make me angry enough to hit them like my stepdad had hit me. I really was afraid. And I hated it.

Now seeing that I was indeed fearful, I began searching for the reason why. How do I overcome something that happens without thought? How do I prevent something that begins without conscious effort? It was like muscle memory, a reaction, a defense that I had set up many years ago to prevent myself from getting hurt, and I didn't even realize it. But how do I fix it?

From that day on, I began asking myself these and many other hard questions every time I felt anger. Not just when my kids or my wife made me angry, but every time. Each time I asked, I got the same result: I did this to myself. Granted, I did it to protect myself, but somewhere along the way, it changed. The initial protection was good, but it changed somehow. When? Why? How?

I heard someone say that the future is fluid, but knowing what is supposed to happen condemns you to the path you are intent on avoiding. Until you were informed of that possible future—because there are many—the path was still fluid. Once you know of a possible future, the choices you make from that point on, even in an effort to avoid it, lead you to that future.

My fear was created from the suffering and pain of my past. Society tells us that we are products of our environments. Knowing this possible future, I had been trying desperately to avoid it. I would do anything to keep my kids from experiencing the pain, loss, and lack of my childhood. I would do anything, including removing myself from the equation, to keep my wife from knowing the beatings my mother endured and that I was helpless to prevent. I would do anything to prevent myself from being helpless ever again. But knowing this possible future was driving me right to it.

Let's be clear: I have never, and will never, raise a hand to my wife or my kids. But words can be just as painful, and that is where I failed them. I was supposed to be their protector, their teacher, their father, and their friend. Instead, I was their tormentor, dictator, and the worst bully they would ever know. I was becoming the thing I had feared the most: my stepdad.

How could this be? How could I become him? Why? Scott's words had not only opened my eyes; they had also broken me. Everything I thought I knew, all of the effort, all of the sacrifices, all of the time spent. It was all backward. Upside down. I was ashamed. Everything I had ever done or said to my wife and kids was running through my head like a horror film. Daily! What do I do? How do I stop what is apparently inevitable? Is it inevitable that I become what I desperately do not want to be?

But God!

> *"Have faith in God,"* Jesus answered. *"Truly I tell you, if anyone says to this mountain, 'Go, throw yourself into the sea,' and does not doubt in their heart but believes that what they say will happen, it will be done for them. Therefore I tell you, whatever you ask for in prayer, believe that you have received it, and it will be yours. And when you stand praying, if you hold anything against anyone, forgive them, so that your Father in heaven may forgive you your sins."*
> **Mark 11:22-25 (NIV)**

He who formed me, named me, and loved me before I was known to anyone had shown me a better future. One in which, if I believed in Him, all things would be possible. I only needed to do two things: forgive my stepdad and forgive myself. Forgiving my stepdad didn't take too long. A lot of prayer. A lot of introspection at who I had become in spite of, and also because of, him. Acceptance of the fact that while his actions caused pain, my actions are my own. I am not him unless I choose to be. Right there! That was it! The fear I was battling was a choice. I was playing with my fear like a paddle ball. I didn't want it, but I had tied myself to it. Every time I tried to toss it away, it just came back. Then as I began to get frustrated with it not going away, I began to hit at it harder and harder, but it would only come right back and usually knock me down. I wasn't letting go.

Letting Go

God's revelation that I was holding on finally allowed me to let it go. All of the pain, the hurt, the hate, everything that was not life-giving that I had chosen to make a part of me was suddenly gone. At that moment, I was no longer broken. I was made new! Why I had never known God this way before confounded me. I had been in church most of my life. Attended services twice every Sunday. Every Wednesday. Pretty much if the doors were open, we were there. Most of the time, I felt like an unwilling participant in the experiments of a mad scientist. Why, after all these years, did God suddenly show up in my life?

Because I finally let Him.

It was no accident. This kind of thing doesn't just happen, does it? Had I been carrying this around all of those years and never knew it? Could I have been free as a child, while still experiencing this pain, but I chose to hate instead? I didn't feel like I was choosing to hate. If anything, I felt like I would give anything to get away from the situation, not latch on to it and hate it the entire time. But I did. Not knowing I had a hold of the business end of a bad thing, I latched on and would not let go. It was as if I were trapped in a cave in the dark and, having grabbed hold of what I thought was the line leading me to the way out, had grabbed hold of a tiger's tail instead. I'm sure both will get you out of the cave, but both have very different ways out.

Having let go of my past, God began to lead me into His future. He began to show me things I had not known before. He placed a desire in my heart to know Him. To read His Word. To seek His will. This new path was not only laid out in front of me but made clear. I had a deep desire to follow it, and I still do.

God began to show me that I was not merely a product of the sum of my past mistakes, problems, pains, and hurts, but instead a child of the most powerful being in existence. Ever! How can that be? I am nothing. I have no real value. I have nothing to offer. Why me?

God is still showing me that answer. But for now, He has shown me the path. The way to Him that most of us seek. A way through our trials, with the least pain and as little loss as possible. It is the purpose of this book to attempt to reveal this path to you in a clear and understandable way. And, with God's help, I will do my best to do so. As I move forward in this task, I pray that God uses His words, His ideas, and His will to open my mind and yours. That both our hearts will be moved by a desire to become closer to Him so that we might heal through forgiveness and relationship. It is a journey that begins with purpose, understanding, wisdom, and knowledge of who He is to us so that through Him we can finally get to know the strangers we have lived with our entire lives: ourselves.

Chapter 2
BELIEVE

He came into the very world he created, but the world didn't recognize him. He came to his own people, and even they rejected him. But to all who believed him and accepted him, he gave the right to become children of God. They are reborn—not with a physical birth resulting from human passion or plan, but a birth that comes from God.
John 1:10-13 (NLT)

Believing is not as easy as it sounds, but also not as difficult as we make it. As a society, our unique cultures have different ways of describing belief and what it means to believe. The way I was taught was the same way you might believe in Santa Claus or aliens. Yes, I said aliens. But for a good reason. You see, I have a hard time looking up at the stars and "believing" we are alone in the universe. I am not saying I believe in little green men, but something has to be out there. Doesn't it?

To me, believing is different than knowledge of a thing's existence. For example, I know that air exists, even though I have never seen it. And I know that the ocean is deep, even though I have never been to the bottom. Why? Because I can breathe the air for survival. I can see smoke moving and feel the wind against my skin in the direction the smoke is traveling. There is scientific evidence that the ocean is deep and that there are creatures living down there that perhaps we have never seen before. But we can believe they exist because of certain evidence.

I am going to stop right here and let you, the reader, know that this is not an attempt to force a non-believer to believe. Or prove to the atheist that there is a God. You are entitled to your opinion, and I truly hope you find happiness and fulfillment in all that you do. However, I do believe that God exists, and the rest of this book should help you understand how I jumped to that conclusion.

I remember sitting in a field when I was a young boy, staring at the trees and the bright blue sky. Watching the wisps of white clouds scattered throughout the sky floating effortlessly overhead. I remember wondering how these clouds came to be. Why was the sky such a pretty shade of blue? How were the birds able to fly? Where did the wind come from? Where does it go when it is not blowing against my face? So many questions about the trees and why they were green, why my dog was so happy to just be even after being run over by a car (for the third time), and what else was out there beyond the blue. Growing up in the country, the night sky was an even more awesome sight to see. A plethora of stars, each seemingly brighter than the next and so many that it looked as though you could just reach up and scoop them out of the sky with your hand. This created a whole new set of questions without answers. Why are there so many? Are we alone? Who made them?

In school, we were taught that these things just suddenly came into being, that there was an explosion of "something" and everything just started growing, each evolving from the former and adapting to the environments that they were presented with. I do not have an issue with this as science can prove that microevolution happens. The age of everything is also not a real issue for me. You see, in my view of religion, science keeps backing up what my Bible says. In the beginning, God created everything from the beginning to the end, the heavens and the earth, and everything on and in them. In my view, this all happened at the same time. My Bible talks about the six days of creation, but it also describes God as a being who is in all places and times at the same time. This indicates to me something that science refers to as "non-linear." If God is omnipotent and omniscient, then the description of the six days of creation was so that we could understand it and nothing else.

In order to understand why I "believe" God exists, we have to talk about what I thought I "knew" about God first. I thought I knew that God created everything. I thought I knew that God was in everything. I thought I knew that God was right there beside me every day and every step of the way. Then troubles came, and I could not see, hear, or find God.

In the middle of my struggles and fears, it was almost impossible to see God in any of it, much less see Him standing next to me. When I was in the worst home situation of my life, I lost my grandmother, the one who held me on the bad days and let me know everything was going to be ok. She was suddenly diagnosed with lung cancer, and within a few months, she was gone, leaving me alone with my pain. Then I was moved away from the only stable situation I had ever known to a new place and I literally had no one to share with.

Then things compounded. I found myself married, going through trials, and my grandfather who may as well have been my dad and whom I was leaning on for the solutions to marriage and relationships, developed a blood disorder and was gone in less than two years. My children were younger than five, and I had no idea what to do with them. How do I treat them? How do I treat my wife? I had so many questions, and who was I going to ask? I was crushed. I felt alone, lost, and adrift in the sea of my life in what appeared to be a category ten hurricane.

To top it off, and within a decade of losing one grandfather—though, despite it all, I had decided to turn back to God and while I was still seeking His will for my life—the last bastion of manhood and knowledge in my life, my other grandfather, my other pillar, was gone in two days, at Christmas no less. The questions that welled up inside my mind were almost overwhelming. How was I supposed to trust God when everything and everyone I was leaning on were being taken away from me? I looked at God and asked, "How am I supposed to trust you? Everything that anchored me from my fear and pain is gone. Taken from me. Why are you doing this to me when I am desperately trying to follow you? Every lighthouse I had is gone!"

Allow me to explain.

Grandmother

When I was twelve years old, my life was the height of what would be a decade-long struggle with abuse. We were living in a house my mother had found, which she had paid to have moved to a piece of property her grandfather had provided. At the time, nearly all of my family lived on the same twenty-four acres of land. We were all close, and my cousins and I spent summers together wandering through the fields, playing games, building forts, and getting into trouble you can only get into in the country.

At home, my mother, whom I regard as a saint even to this day and the very first angel in my life, was doing her best to keep it together. On her third marriage, and worst husband, she endured beatings I could never imagine. Sometimes she would take the beating instead of me and sometimes because of me. My stepdad had very strict ideas of how life should be, mostly his, and any deviation from that idea was met swiftly and oftentimes brutally. My sister and I were hit with everything from switches to two-by-fours. The latter was not a fun experience.

I remember that night like it was yesterday. I do not remember what I did to trigger these events, though I have tried. The result, however, I will never forget. The house we were having moved was on site, but under construction. We drove out there for some reason, and by the time we arrived, I was in trouble. I was dragged from the car into the house in the dark, and no one was around for about 400 yards and inside their own houses. I was scared.

Chapter 2: Believe

Once in the house, my stepdad realized he had no belt and couldn't find an extension cord. Even more angered by these events, he picked up a two-by-four and began to walk toward me. I began to scream and beg that he spare me. I bargained with him to "just give me another chance and I will behave." This all may as well have fallen on deaf ears as he continued to walk toward me. As he raised the board, wound up like he was Babe Ruth, and began to hit me with it, I began to scream as loud as I could.

I would prove to be a much harder target to hit than I'm sure he initially thought, and by the time he hit me the third time, I saw headlights shining into the house from the outside. I didn't know who it was, and I didn't care. I hoped this reprieve would be just enough for him to calm down and either continue the beating at home with something else or hopefully end it completely. I soon discovered that this interloper was my mother's cousin who lived down the road. Somehow, from inside her house more than 400 yards away and over the sound of her TV, she had heard my screams. God was there.

My mother, on the other hand, was quite often kicked, punched, and thrown on just about every occasion that angered him. I assumed thrashing some less-capable individuals somehow made him feel better, but it did not seem to reduce the frequency or intensity of the ones that followed. And it was during these times that I could go and stay with either of my grandparents and experience a reprieve from that life. It was like living two lives. Superheroes began to be my solace. Comic books and movies were among the very long list of things I was not allowed to participate in per my mother's chosen religion at the time. Those comic books and movies were the only way I could escape the world that I had no choice but to live in, and it was those weird rules of religion that would later drive a wedge between God and me.

My mother's parents were on the same property we lived on, and so I frequently ran to them. My grandparents all knew that my home life was less than desirable, but they had absolutely no idea to what extent. It wasn't until the night my stepdad took the two-by-four to me that they got even a small idea. You see, for some reason, we believe that if someone is mistreating us, it is somehow our fault. That the abuse was not only caused by us, but somehow we asked for it and are thereafter ashamed of what "we" have done. What a load of crap.

It wasn't long after this that my grandmother (my mother's mom) was diagnosed with lung cancer. My two grandmothers are both amazing women. They taught me lots of things, but most of all, they taught me what it looked like to be loved, truly loved, by a woman. My mother loved me, and I her, but she has also had to deal with the hurt of being beaten every day by a man, and as I got older, I was becoming the thing that hurt her the most: a man.

My grandmothers had no such predisposition and therefore simply loved and cared for me without cause or requirement. It was this kind of love that I would later apply to my relationship with my wife. But it did not help to soften the blow when my maternal grandmother passed. I remember that night, from the call at home telling us to come to the hospital, to the moments after she had gone. The only word I could use to describe that night: devastating. They say that life goes on, and in a way it does. But, that night—that night lingers in my mind even to this day. Writing this only makes it that much more prevalent in my mind. A love lost, a voice silenced, and lives changed forever.

Believe it or not, God was there. He was there during the beatings. He was there when my grandmother was diagnosed with cancer, and He was there when she died. Looking back, I wish I had the relationship I have with Him now so I could have embraced Him and experienced the peace He now provides. I would have danced in His presence while the angels sang praises that my grandmother's soul was joined with them in heaven. You see, in her last days, my mother was busy sharing God's peace, love, and joy with her. My mother—yes, the one being beaten up almost daily—had peace and joy that I could not explain. She had drawn so close to God in that time of her life that He would literally give her whatever she asked for.

I remember being in the car with her one night on a very dark, very long country road and the car fuel gauge needle pointing at E. I remember my mother praying to God so loudly and so intensely. It was both frightening and powerful. I remember intently watching that fuel gauge as she prayed, both expectant and doubtful at the same time. However, to both my joy and surprise, I watched that needle go from E to ¼ in the middle of her prayer. So yes, my mother could, and can, call down heaven with just her words, and she was sharing that with her mom in her darkest hour. My grandmother, through my mother's testimony, came to know God that month, and so when she passed, I believe there were angels singing and that God personally came to welcome her home. This wasn't the last time God was present for my worst either.

The Fight

It would be four years and several moves later that my stepdad and I would finally come to blows for the first time. Having moved so many times since I had started school, relationships with other people my own age were not easy to form. Relationships in general were not easy to form. Think about it: why make friends you're just going to have to say goodbye to? Why try?

Just a few months into our most recent move, tensions were high. It was arguably the nicest place I had lived to date, with the exception of my grandparents' home, and the violence was more rare now that I was about to become a teenager. My stepdad had become much more picky, and the roles my sister and I had begun to fill were more that of maid and butler than anything else. The difference was that when our work did not meet his very particular standards, we were reminded quite swiftly, and violently, that we had done it wrong.

The day of the first fight, my sister and I, being kids, had come home from school with some of our friends from the neighborhood and we were having fun. We never left our yard, but we also had not done our chores. Realizing that time was almost up, and our stepdad would be home from work very soon, we enlisted the help of our friends.

I know I said it was difficult to make friends, but there are some people in this world who you are just meant to be connected to. These were some of those people, and we are still friends with them to this day. Our particular lives do not intersect as often as we would like, but when we see each other, it is like family. We carry on as if we haven't missed a beat. That is, in my opinion, a true friendship. Never mind the fact that they helped us clean our dishes, fold the laundry, and sweep and mop the floors, among other things that afternoon. There truly are not words to describe how awesome these friends are. And again, God was there. The reason wouldn't be clear until I met my wife.

Ten years later, I found out that the friends I had been spending time with every day after school, on weekends, and most of the summer had a mutual friend: my future wife. You have to understand, though, that she grew up in Houston, Texas. My friends and I lived in a tiny little town in South Texas called LaWard. Only 115 people lived there. That included me. My future wife went to church with these friends' uncle. She was friends with their cousin and would visit LaWard with their cousin some summers. We had never met because those same visits were when I was having my summer visits with my grandparents. It was these friends who were helping us clean that day. God was definitely working.

Together we had that house so clean you could see your reflection in the countertops. It smelled of cleaners, and the laundry had been separated, folded, hung, and put away before our stepdad pulled into the driveway. He walked into the entryway, took off his work boots, took off his socks, and proceeded to walk through the kitchen barefoot. He inspected the counters, noted the laundry was no longer in the entry near the washer and dryer, and noted all of the dishes were clean and put away (none left out drying in the rack). As he walked across the kitchen floor, which we had cleaned in the method he required, on hands and knees with a scrub brush and a towel to dry it, he would stop and pick up his sweaty feet and check to see if he picked up any dirt from the floor. He had made it almost entirely through the kitchen and was just about to the carpet when he found a few grains of dirt on his foot. When we saw this, my sister and I both looked at each other, and when our eyes locked, we both thought the same thing, Oh crap!

Our mother had been home for about half an hour and had actually been helping us finish the laundry. Our friends had gone home when she arrived, and it was just us in the house when he had pulled up. The house we lived in was at least one block from anything on either side, and so the noise that was about to emanate from our house wasn't going to disturb anyone or anything except a few birds, some snakes, and a whole lot of bugs. Needless to say, when he found that dirt on his foot, he began the most verbally abusive tirade I have ever been privy to or part of. We were called names that would make a sailor blush. There was nothing we were or ever would be good at. Apparently, your appearance is a reason you do poorly at things because we were not going to have good-looking spouses because we were never going to be good-looking enough or smart enough to do so. He was in the middle of berating us even further when my mother, hearing enough, came in to defend us. Uh oh!

When my mother arrived in the room, she began to tell him in no uncertain terms that he would not be allowed to talk to "her" children that way anymore. That we had worked hard to make sure he got what he had asked for and it was not fair to speak to us that way after such an effort. She wasn't wrong. That house was cleaner than it had ever been that night, but he was going to have none of it. This woman was not going to stand in his face and make him less of a man in front of his subordinates. He had already done that for himself.

As the yelling grew louder, my sister and I knew what was going to happen next and began begging Mom to back down. She did not. Wap! That was the sound of his big, burly open hand slamming across the side of my mother's face. Then he grabbed her by the shirt and hair and began to throw her around the kitchen like a ragdoll, yelling obscenities and letting her know beyond a doubt that he was the man and that if she wanted to help us, she was going to be the mop. He was going to be the one doing the mopping.

Standing back watching this as my sister desperately tried to pry his hands off of our mother and failed miserably, something changed inside me. The years of being told how worthless I was, how weak I was, and how useless I would always be faded into the background. What grew inside me was a determination that this interloper, this pretender, this person who claims to have control in MY home and torments MY family, who uses and takes over and over again until there is nothing left, was not going to take anything else from us. This was going to stop, and it was going to stop NOW!

You might be thinking that my first thought was to just rush in and give him the beating he deserved and that, bloodied and bruised, he would tuck tail and run, but no. I was still under the impression that I was weaker than he was. I still thought I had no chance to succeed. My plan for him was much worse. As he struck my mother yet again, I decided his life was worth less than mine and that the only way to save my family's lives was to end his.

The only way around the three of them fighting in the doorway was to jump over a chair to get to the door to the kitchen. The door was open, and I could see the gleaming knife in the knife block on the kitchen counter. I just knew, without doubt, that if I could reach that knife, I would simply turn around and plunge it full force into his back and it would all be over. Sure, I may have to go to jail, but my mother and sister would be safe. This was the plan. I never made it to the kitchen.

As I jumped over the chair, my foot caught the back and I stumbled. I did not fall, but the hesitation in my approach to the knife let him know where I was going, and with his large right hand, he reached back, grabbed me by the collar, and pulled me into the fray. The one place I did not want to be. The place that I felt I could never succeed. The place where my fear lived. And now, I was standing right in front of it. The difference was that, this time, I had had enough.

I was being reeled in backward by my stepdad, who, by the way, was more than one hundred pounds heavier than me. He was also an amateur arm wrestler who spent many years in the oil fields slinging pipe. And he was about the size of a small car. For me, it felt like I had tried to run past the mouth of a lion and failed. But in that moment, a feeling I had never felt before began to rise up inside of me. I suddenly felt like I could do anything. It really felt like I had the power to rip off his head and feed it to him. Whether you call that a Daniel moment or Samson being reincarnated inside of me, it doesn't matter. In that moment, with that feeling, I was able to make a decision. Fight!

Almost pulled into his hold, I reached back with both hands, grabbed him by the throat, wrapped my arms around his thick neck, and, like a reflex, pulled as hard and as fast as I could over my shoulder. With my hip pressed into his thigh, he came up off of his feet and flew over my shoulder. But I did not let go of his neck. And, as he came down on top of my body, it felt as though I had just dropped a fridge on myself, but I maintained my grip around his neck.

In a headlock administered by me and shocked and disoriented by what was happening, he tried without success to free himself. I was in just the right position to maintain my hold but not be hit. He could not reach me. I began to get tunnel vision. Squeezing as hard as I could, I was not letting this beast get up. If I did, I was done for, with my mother and sister to follow. As the tunnel vision grew to near blindness, I realized I could not hear anything either. This became noticeable when I saw the silhouette of my mother standing over us. She appeared to be yelling at me. I heard nothing.

As I attempted to hear what my mother was saying, my vision also began to return. The trouble was that as my senses returned, I began to hear my mother's words and noticed I was starting to weaken. "Let him go! You're killing him!" my mother was yelling. She was just repeating it over and over. As this began to sink in, I realized that my stepdad was a peculiar shade of purple from the neck up. Was I really doing it? Was I winning? Were we going to be free of him? Finally?! Then came the question, "Could I actually take another man's life?"

The realization that I, no matter how much I wanted to, could not take another man's life hit me in the face like a bag of flour. It deflated every feeling I had all at the same time. Overwhelmed with rage, and realizing I was beginning to lose my grip, I needed to make another decision. Do I let him go or kill him? It was a very unique place to be. Holding another man's life in my hands, I could just squeeze harder, for just a few seconds longer, and he would be gone. But, like David, I could not kill Saul. He was the appointed ruler over me, and just having my hands on him was wrong. I am not David, and he was not a king, but in that moment, the thought that I had overstepped my place was going through my head. So I let go. God was there.

He immediately jumped up from my grasp and literally ran to his bedroom and locked the door. My mother, tears streaming from her face, stood over me with a look of terror, pride, and love. My family was safe. Did I just do that? Was I strong enough to defeat a giant? How? As my mother, sister, and I embraced each other and sobbed, I wondered if he would leave after this or if it was going to get worse. My stepdad did not leave his room for the rest of the night.

In the morning, I awoke to silence. Trepidatious as to what awaited me outside my bedroom door, I waited for a while and just listened. No voices, no sobbing, nothing. What was going on? I walked slowly from my room to the kitchen, where I found my mother sitting at the table, head in hand. "He's gone," she said. "I don't think he's coming back. He took most of his stuff and said he would get the rest in a few weeks. I don't know what we are going to do." At that moment, I wondered, did I do something wrong? My mother was sad that this monster of a man was gone. Why? And so we moved.

A few weeks before moving into the new place, my stepdad showed up. The two of them seemed to have made amends; I was not thrilled. I was cautious. I was hesitant. I was terrified. He, however, seemed to have changed his tune. Same bird, different song. He avoided me as much as possible. He was more gentle with my sister than before. There was no fighting, no yelling, and no violence. I was not impressed.

When moving into the new place, an apartment, the sweet exterior began to dissolve and I saw it. While moving boxes from the U-Haul to

Chapter 2: Believe

the apartment, this "changed man" began making demands. Unhappy with my efforts to unload his crap, he began giving me multiple tasks and expecting me to complete them all at the same time. If the tasks were all in the same room, I may have been able to pull it off. These were not. He was looking for trouble. In the middle of one of his quiet tirades, I had another feeling of indignation. I was not going to be talked to like this anymore. I overpowered you once; I'll do it again.

I began to stand up to this bully and let him know in no certain terms that he was being unfair, and he either needed to be patient and let me finish or do it himself. His reaction was exactly what I expected; mine was not. He rushed at me with a look of hate and anger mixed to an explosive end. I stood my ground. As he got closer, I dug my feet in, turned my hips into a fighting stance, raised my fists, swung, and chickened out mid-swing. Uh oh!

He absorbed my weak punch and grabbed hold of my throat with one hand. He pushed me backward on my heels and walked me backward and off balance; I knew this was the end. I kicked, punched, and wrestled as hard as I could, but I was a bird in a bear trap. As his grip on my throat began to intensify, I lost my balance as he pushed me against the couch. I collapsed backward onto the couch as his hand grabbed the back of my head, gripped my hair, and pulled. As I fell, he pulled my head back so far that I landed on my face. When I did, the back of my head tapped my shoulder blades and I could not breathe. Between his monster hand squeezing my neck and the sharp angle and position of my head, my windpipe was closed for business.

My mother, having walked in to see all of this, was punching him and screaming at him to let me go while I, "the big man," was helpless and all but paralyzed under this car of a man. Eventually she managed to get him to lose interest in killing me, and he released his grip on my neck. I assume he realized this was going to be a regular event between us, because while I was recovering from my near-death experience, he moved out. It has been nearly thirty years since that night, and I have not seen him since, except for pictures. That night, God was there.

No God

These events eventually led me to believe that there was no God. How could a God let all of these bad things happen to someone who, at least at the time, had been doing everything he could to be a faithful believer? I was praying, reading my Bible, going to church, and actively trying to be a better person despite my circumstances. Still I had to go through hell for what felt like no reason. And in the middle of that, my grandmother died, my friends were miles away, and I had no one to talk to or be encouraged by. I had no structure, no path, no purpose. This sucks!

I began to do things I normally would not have done. I stopped going to church. I was more flirtatious with girls—not that it changed anything. I was still perpetually single. It was as if my stepdad was a prophet, and this was just the life I needed to be resigned to living. Alone. No matter what I did or said, I could not get a date. Girls would talk to me, laugh with me, even hang out with me. When the question "Will you go out with me?" came up, they were gone.

As I began my last year of high school, we were living in Houston, and I discovered that the private school my mother had worked so very hard to put me in was going to result in a GED equivalent. Not even a GED. I stayed in school and put up with the bullies and the BS associated with the religious rules that caused me so much hell in school. These rules ostracized me and made me an outcast. I was good, really good at baseball, but I was not allowed to play organized sports. I was exceptionally strong, deceptively so. I was six feet tall and one hundred forty-five pounds. Even so, I could deadlift three hundred pounds like it was nothing. I could bench press almost two hundred pounds, and I had never worked out a day in my teenage life. But I couldn't be on the powerlifting team because sports were the devil's playground. It was like everything that was going to get me any type of positive attention was against our religion. Why?

There were a plethora of people we went to church with, or knew at other churches in our organization, who would say and do one thing at church, and then when they weren't paying attention, you would catch them doing the opposite. It was ok to tell you that what you wanted was a sin, but that same thing was ok when they wanted it. What was this backward, selfish, non-Christ-like attitude that seemed to be pervasive in the world that I lived in? Insert judgments here. It was all happening, and it made no sense. This is not the God, the Christ, or the Christians that I had been taught about since I was three. I was out.

I left school, left home, moved back to my hometown, and got a job. I had an uncle who was kind enough to let me live with him as long as I had a job. He didn't charge me rent or anything; he just wanted me to have a job. He was my aunt's ex-husband and my cousin's father and not even blood related to me, but he treated me like I was. And I appreciated it. I got a job working at his shop and continued my downward spiral until it broke me. I drank, did drugs, partied, and lied. Not too much was off limits.

Eventually, my cousin and I moved out of my uncle's house, me first and then my cousin. I moved in with another cousin, where my illicit proclivities began to evolve. I was still single and still a virgin. I was seventeen and figured I needed to solve this itch I had. I began a year-and-a-half long attempt to have as much sex as I could. Little did I know that the way women are portrayed in porn is not how they actually are. If you find one who is, you probably want to keep your parts away from hers.

I spent the next eighteen months trying everything I could think of to get a girl to notice me sexually. I changed my appearance. I offered to buy their drugs and their alcohol and drove them and their friends places. I was pathetic, and they knew it. But who's going to turn down free stuff?

This continued shamefully until someone I knew when I was a kid, who had a similar disgust with church and who was following the same path I was, began to hang out with me. He knew some girls who apparently didn't say no and made the introductions. Looking back, I was lucky the first time not to catch anything I could not wash off.

As this behavior continued, I deserved to catch something, but I didn't. I was playing Russian roulette with my life, and it never dawned on me. Although I had to go through some major and well-deserved drama, I finally decided that life was going to get me killed. God or no God, I could not live like that. I had spent most of my life living in fear; I wasn't going to volunteer for more. God was there.

It should be said that these young women were just as lost as I was. Nothing about what they were doing was any more or less sinful than my own thoughts and actions. If I could go back in time, I would rather have invited them to church than to my bed. I have no idea what was going through their minds or why they chose to do what they did. I know exactly what was going through mine. I only pray that God led, or is leading, them to Him. If they read this book, may the words of my story bring them peace and a path to the freedom that a life with God offers. I also pray that they find it in their hearts to forgive me for not treating them like the women they were called to be. And yes, we are all called.

Ending my search for love by the night, I decided to also end my drug use and alcohol consumption. I called my mom in Houston and asked if she still had room for me in her home. She was remarried now to her fourth husband, who, by all my experiences, was a nice guy. Maybe a bit clingy, but nice. Not that clingy is necessarily a bad thing; we were just not used to clingy, much less nice, and I knew my mother was struggling with it. But the violence was over. My mother, knowing some of what I had been up to for the last eighteen months, welcomed me into their home without question, and so did he. To be honest, it was like I had never left. The prodigal returned. God was there.

The One

One stipulation of my return was that I had to find a job, and I had to go to church. With a skater haircut and a newly installed earring, church was the last place I felt welcome, especially the churches my mom went to. But, a deal is a deal, and so to church I went. Skater cut and earring too. Oh the looks. The stares. It was as if I had walked into

Chapter 2: Believe

a country and western bar wearing a dress. Most of them aren't going to do anything to you, but they all want you to leave. If you're lucky, the ones that do want to do something won't. That was church, but God was there.

That first service back, my mother wanted me to sit with her because there was a girl she wanted to introduce me to that night, but I made it clear that I was never going to date anyone my mother hooked me up with for multiple reasons. As we walked in, and I endured the stares and silent judgment, I let my mother know that a seat near the back would be fine. Normally sitting toward the front, she and her husband agreed that we could sit toward the back to accommodate my discomfort. The girl my mom wanted me to meet was not there that night, much to my relief.

The service started as most of them did with music, singing, and an offering plate being passed around. I remember thinking that these arrogant people would ask a homeless man for money if he made the mistake of walking into their service. I remember that service because, during the offering, a few of the members got up on the podium and presented the preacher with the keys to a brand-new Lincoln Navigator. I thought, "This church is in such a poor neighborhood, and the money you have been collecting couldn't be used for a better purpose than to schmooze the pastor?" This was one of many bad attitudes and opinions I had for the next eight years. I hated church, and this display was making it worse.

My bad attitude and opinions aside, I still tried to do what I could to make my mother happy. I tried to get back into church, and so I began hanging out with some of the youth there. They seemed pretty cool, and I began to make friends. I also began to get closer to God again and found myself praying. I was actually starting to enjoy the experience. That was when it happened.

At church, I had begun to sit closer to the front with some of the friends I had made, without my family. One night, I was sitting in the pew, and as the service started, the choir began to file in. As the first song started, I saw her. The one. It was a feeling I had never felt before. I had no idea who she was, where she came from, or how long she had been going to this church. I had never seen her before. But I couldn't see enough. Not in a carnal way either. She was the most beautiful thing I had ever seen. It looked like she was backlit by the stars, and even though there were other pretty girls standing right beside her, it was as if she were the only one.

I felt as though I had known her my entire life. Like we had been friends forever and she had just been gone and suddenly returned. The joy that enveloped my being was indescribable. She was the most beautiful creature I had ever seen. I needed to know her name. I asked my friends who this girl was, and they told me. One even made the introduction after service. Leaning against the wall in the church's foyer, skater cut and all, I made the biggest fool of myself ever, and she didn't notice. Oh she noticed me, but to her, I was not a fool. In her eyes was my future and I needed to see more. Luckily for me, she invited my friend and I to go have dinner with her group.

At dinner, she sat across from me and right between my two friends, who both apparently had crushes on her. At one point during the evening, as all of us youth were sitting separately from the adults, a game of spin the bottle was suggested, but we had no bottle. I suggested we use a butter knife instead. Yes! These were church kids. For the record, I did not suggest the game. I merely thought it was a great idea.

I was so nervous that my sweat was sweating. It was so wrong that I wanted to be near her so badly that I was willing to risk losing her to one of the other guys in a kissing contest rather than be without her for one more second. And so it began: pick a number and the lowest number goes first. I was to go last.

It was painful, watching helplessly as each of the three guys before me got to take their spin. The first one spun and got one of the other girls at the table. The second one spun and got my other buddy sitting there. We all laughed as the two of them negotiated how they were going to handle their awkward first kiss. Cheeks it was, but for a moment, we

Chapter 2: Believe

thought, "Surely they won't." Then came the third, the best looking of us at the time, or so I thought. But I was still broken from my childhood, so Quasimodo would have appeared better looking to me than I would have to me. Although, to be fair, my buddy was a good-looking dude. He spun, and to my horror, it landed on her. Oh no, this is terrible. One kiss from him and I am finished. He leaned in, she looked at me, and ... wait, what? She looked at me! Our eyes connected, and her head turned at the last second, leaving my buddy with just a cheek. What just happened?

Feeling let down, my buddy complained, but he was shot down by nearly every girl at the table and told that it was her choice whether she wanted him to kiss her on the lips or not. She obviously did not. His appeals used up and denied, the turn fell to me. My turn. What if it lands on one of the others? What if I get one of the guys, as my other friend had? So many what ifs. Only one way to find out. I reached out, placed three fingers on the butter knife, and spun, half wanting to close my eyes and half not wanting to miss it. I winced as the knife slowed. When the knife came to rest, it was pointing at—? Who was it pointing at? It was only barely pointing in her direction but not clear enough to be sure. Since it was not clear exactly where it was pointing, she moved over to be in front of it. Is this actually happening?

Certain now that the knife and she had chosen, she leaned over the table to receive her kiss. I chickened out. She was too important for such a cheap kiss. When I didn't lean in to give it, she relaxed, and once her weight was off her hands, I took one and proceeded to look her deeply in the eyes and kiss her hand ever so gently. I lingered just long enough for her to feel the soft warmth of my lips on her hand, but not so long that she felt uncomfortable. This girl is the one. She will know she is the one, and she will always be the one. That thought went through my mind in that moment, as our lives together flashed before my eyes. It was late September. I married her the next July. God was there.

Oh yeah. Guess who my mom had wanted me to meet? Yep, I married her. And do you know what I found? God was there.

The Process

Every journey is a process. Each step is an experience, each trial a lesson, and every victory a blessing. In the middle of that process, it is difficult to see further than the trial. During the trial, every step seems to bring with it even more turmoil. It seems that the storm you are currently enduring is the only thing you will ever know for the rest of your existence. It has been my experience, however, that every storm is temporary. Yes, every storm! The storm may last longer than you want it to, hurt more than you think is fair, and destroy everything you were holding dear. But the storm will end soon enough.

Our ability to persevere is honed in these storms. How we respond to situations that cause pain, how we deal with that pain, and whether we choose to recover from it are part of the journey. It is up to us to rise above the waves or sink beneath them. While in them, I cannot always remember that. It is not easy to ignore trouble. Especially when it affects us personally. While you are tossed about on the sea like a toy, the thunder and lightning seem equally out to get you, and there doesn't seem to be anything good on the horizon. All we tend to see are more dark clouds.

The storm is, however, only a moment in time. Our entire lives on this earth are like the tip of a ballpoint pen, and our storms are tiny specks on the end of that pen. Our perspective as participants causes us to view them larger than ourselves. And even though they are just a fraction of who we are and an even smaller moment of our time, we will inevitably allow our perspective to tower over our logic. But what if I told you that there was a better way? What if I told you that we pretend it doesn't exist?

Perspective. A tricky little thing. On one hand, we are in moments of pain and anguish, and on the other hand, we have absolutely no idea what will happen in the next five minutes, much less tomorrow. Yet we don't hesitate to worry about it. We allow ourselves to be consumed with fear of the unknown and crippled by the thought of what might be. I did it. I still catch myself doing it. I'm pretty sure that we all do it.

The solution: Don't.

In the moments of my life shared in this book so far, my life was at times terrifying. Painful. Sometimes uncertain. There are stories yet to tell. However, hindsight is 20/20, and I can see now that God was there. The better way was standing right beside me, protecting me.

You might say, "But you were beaten!" and I will say, "But I did not die." Or you might say, "You lost the ones closest to you when you needed them most." But I would still say, "For everyone I lost, God gave me two more." You might even read these stories and say, "You grew up broken and lost." And my answer would be, "So that God could teach me how to be the best version of myself that I could be. No frills. No gimmicks. Just the truth." How can I look at each of these situations and find joy instead of pain, purpose instead of tragedy, and blessing rather than loss? Because I believe!

> Jesus performed many other signs in the presence of his disciples, which are not recorded in this book. But these are written that you may believe that Jesus is the Messiah, the Son of God, and that by believing you may have life in his name.
> **John 20:30-31 (NIV)**

The Bible contains many Scriptures regarding belief. In most, belief is described as the starting place for faith. In fact, when Paul and Silas were in prison, the jailer asked them what he must do to be saved. Their answer, "Believe in the Lord Jesus, and you will be saved" (**Acts 16:31 NIV**). But it doesn't end there. They also add that if he believed in Jesus, the jailer and his entire household would be saved.

Belief. The only thing "required" to be saved.

In another story, Jesus was about to raise the deceased child of a synagogue leader, Jairus. Those who had come to where Jesus and Jairus were had told Jairus that he should not bother Jesus anymore because his once-sick daughter was now dead, and there was no reason to try to get Him to heal her. But Jesus, overhearing what they were telling Jairus, told them, *"Don't be afraid; just believe"* (**Mark 5:36 NIV**).

Believe? The child was dead. Don't we need faith, or some miracle, at this point? Jesus simply instructed Jairus to have no fear and believe. When Jairus did as Jesus asked, Jesus took Jairus, his wife, Peter, James, and John and went into where the deceased child was. When they were alone in the room, all Jesus said was, *"Little girl, I say to you, get up!"* (**Mark 5:41 NIV**). The Bible says that immediately, she got up and began walking around. Jairus and his wife, who had just witnessed this miracle, were astonished. The original Greek actually translates as "beside themselves in awe and wonder," so-called speechless, if you will. All that was required of them was that they simply believed that a miracle would happen. That Jesus could change what had already happened. And they did.

What I believe God has shown me throughout my life so far is that even in the trials, He is there. He has shown me this because He needs me to believe. Why? Because He has called us to be light unto the world. A guide for those who may not be able to see the path. And those who can believe can be used by God to reach those who may be lost. He has called all of us by name, from the beginning of time. He has loved all of us from before we were born. And as we become imitators of Christ, we begin to welcome the message He brings, even in the midst of our suffering, with joy given to us by the Holy Spirit. All we have to do to get there is believe.

> For we know, brothers and sisters loved by God, that he has chosen you, because our gospel came to you not simply with words but also with power, with the Holy Spirit and deep conviction. You know how we lived among you for your sake. You became imitators of us and of the Lord, for you welcomed the message in the midst of severe suffering with the joy given by the Holy Spirit. And so you became a model to all the believers in Macedonia and Achaia.
> **1 Thessalonians 1:4-7 (NIV)**

Chapter 3
FAITH

The Secret

> Now faith is the substance of things hoped for,
> the evidence of things not seen.
> **Hebrews 11:1 (NKJV)**

Many of us have heard of or know this verse by heart. It is used quite often and usually to emphasize some message about faith that is being delivered. What most of us do not know is that faith is more, so much more. What we also do not know is that in this one verse lies a secret to changing our lives. A secret that, once understood, can and will change the very foundation of who you and I are.

Language is a very important and often difficult thing to understand. We try to make it simple. And most of us want others to understand not just what we are saying and writing, but also our intentions in doing so. We all desire to know, be known, and be understood. It is this longing for community that draws us together, but it is also the thing that drives us apart.

I may understand a topic, idea, or word in one way, while another could have a similar or altogether different understanding. This uncertainty can, and often does, cause animosity, distrust, and confusion among us. That is why the search for knowledge and understanding is so very important.

Solomon, the world's wisest known individual, wrote in **Proverbs 18:15 (NIV)**, "The heart of the discerning acquires knowledge, for the ears of the wise seek it out." This declaration is simple to understand. It states that if you are wise, you will naturally seek more knowledge and seek to understand the world around you. You will do this so that you can discern, or be able to know when you are being lied to, and know the difference between truth and lies, fact and fiction. Seeking knowledge allows you to know when someone is trying to inform you or deceive you. Your knowledge of the world and languages around you can keep you from being taken advantage of, but it can also allow you to help someone else untangle themselves from the fiction they may already believe and find truth.

The secret hidden in **Hebrews 11:1** is that the Greek word translated as substance also has another meaning. Several, actually. Having been in church most of my life, I had struggled with such a vague way of describing faith. Substance? Faith is anything, and everything, all around me and inside of me, even a part of me? Yes! But what exactly is it? Where does it come from? How do I use it? What does it do? All of these questions were longing to be answered, welling up inside of me, and choking me with uncertainty. Clouding my judgment. Turning into doubt. Why? Because I was not seeking knowledge.

It has become my understanding that when God places a question, a desire, or a task in your heart, you cannot eat, sleep, or live without thinking about it. Your life and everything in it becomes consumed by what God has placed there. He is a "consuming fire" (**see Hebrews 12:29 NIV**). We cannot help but burn with that fire. And if we do nothing about it, we will begin to die on the inside. We die because we begin to find ourselves growing cold. We are not doing what God has called us to do. We are not following or seeking His will. And so we die. Just as a plant out of the soil or a fish out of water. We cannot sustain ourselves without His purpose, His grace, and His joy. When we try, we fail. Most of the time, we take others with us. Our family suffers, our friends suffer, and we suffer. All because we choose to ignore what God has called and created us for.

That one thing that we cannot do without is knowledge. Without knowledge, we are easily swayed. Without knowledge, we are puppets. We can be made to do, or repeat, anything that someone with more knowledge wants us to. Why? Because the words they speak tickle our ears. They sound good. Their words have facts in them; they keep us just close enough to what we think we know and pepper in just enough truth to make it a reality for us. Because we don't know any better.

When we seek out our own knowledge, our belief is affected. How? It is strengthened by purpose, identity, and understanding. The one person you trust most in this world is yourself. If you picked up your Bible, and you studied the languages it was written in, and you fit your life and circumstances into what you were reading, wouldn't you feel better about what you believed? God revealed this to me as I sat in a church service with no Bible, no notes, just taking the preacher's word for it. The question He asked me in that moment was, "How does it feel being a pawn?" This sparked an entire discussion with my inner man and with God. The end result: a profound quest and hunger for knowledge.

Seek and You Will Find

At the age of thirty-five, I began two years of theological study. Everything before this and since has been God teaching me, revealing the flaws, and shaping who I am to become. He has grown in me a desire to know more. He has placed questions in my mind and the expectation that He will answer them. Questions like: Why does the Bible confuse me instead of enlighten me? Why are there so many different doctrines, beliefs, and paths to salvation from the same words? Who is God? Who am I? Who am I to Him?

So I began to dig. I began to seek Him for the first time in my life with everything I could muster. I poured myself into study, and I struggled to keep up. I was running a business that required twelve to eighteen hours of my days seven days a week, and I was still serving in my local church as the media director. I was changing stage designs, going to all of the practices to set sound, and trying to find time with my wife and kids, all while pulling a full course load in my studies.

All of the reading, all of the writing, and all of the discussion with my classmates, who all had their own backgrounds, beliefs, and doctrines, answered as many questions as it created. I began to wonder if all of this was just going to leave me even more confused than I already was. But I persevered. I struggled, I sacrificed, and I cried, but I would not give up. I couldn't. It was as if I was on autopilot and I had no control of the vehicle. I sometimes did not want to keep going. I had so many responsibilities, so many problems, and my past was fighting me every step of the way. Why couldn't I just keep doing things the way I had been? Why couldn't I just be who I had always been? It was working so far. Everyone else was fine with it. Everyone else was doing it. Why not me?

As time passed, the studies began to open my eyes. Not just to how the Bible was written, in what order it was written, and by whom, but I was also reading books like *A Normal Christian Life* by Watchman Nee. The understanding of Scripture that people like Nee were bringing to the table bothered me. Yes, it bothered me. I had been conditioned most of my life to believe Scripture a certain way. I was "told" what it was and how to interpret it. And, until now, I had never heard it differently. I never thought to look either. These new words and ideas were antagonistic, drawing me into discussions and thought processes that I had never considered before. I was breaking free, growing, and I didn't even know it.

These books and discussions were opening a door I had never tried to open. I was being informed of things that my churches and the preachers I had followed were not discussing. Those men and women brought excellent messages; they instilled in me a thorough "fear" of God. They made me aware that the "end" was indeed near and that tomorrow wasn't promised, but they did not tell me how to avoid the inevitable. Sure, they taught about salvation; they taught about the Holy Spirit, righteousness, and forgiveness. They taught about baptism, fasting, giving, and hope. But if I were to deliver those messages to you, would you know the way?

You would probably end up like me, confused and feeling like I was just not good enough for God because I could never reach that place that they all said was the goal. That place with God and the Holy Spirit that would mean I had made it, the proof in the pudding of my salvation: speaking in tongues. Believe it, it is a real thing. Not only have I heard it, but I have seen amazing things happen before, during, and after. I have been present for a lame man getting up and walking—twice. I have witnessed a deaf woman getting her hearing. I have been the recipient of multiple healings, including a diagnosed rupture of my C5 and C6 discs in my neck that were causing excruciating pain. Completely healed! And in Jesus's name when doctors said surgery was the only way. But even with all of that proof of God's existence, and no matter how righteously I tried to live, I could not get to the place in my relationship with God that would allow me to experience that one gift, the one I had been taught was the proof of God's Spirit inside of me: speaking in tongues.

It wasn't until Watchman Nee's book that I realized that something was wrong. I knew something was wrong, but until that book, I thought it was me. *A Normal Christian Life* is a discussion of the book of Romans in The Holy Bible. In it, Watchman Nee discusses the content in the book of Romans and what it means to him, how he understands it, and how he feels God has revealed it to him. His quest for knowledge led him to that understanding. His desire to put on paper what God placed in his heart is what I was both blessed and indignant to read. As I read his words, I found myself arguing with them. The contradiction to my own understanding and lifelong belief was causing feelings that I did not understand. I wanted more than anything for this to stop, and if I could have finished the class without reading this book, I would have. Thank God I could not.

As I read his words, I grew angry with "the lies" I was certain he was telling. His writing did something to me that my entire life in church had not. It made me want to read the Bible. Not for the sake of reading it like I had been raised to believe. That had not created in me a "reason" to waste my time reading an old book written like a Shakespearean play, but this time was different. I had found purpose. I was going to prove that this guy, Watchman Nee, was wrong. No one was going to force me to read a book that was trying to change my belief. No one was going to walk me back from my relationship with God. No one was going to force me to read this blasphemy, and I was going to prove it and save everyone else's soul in that class, including the instructor. I opened my Bible, which I had read through many times, but this time it was different. This time I was actually doing it with my eyes open.

As I read the Scriptures that Watchman Nee was claiming were true and that deviated from my belief, I repeatedly found that not only was he right, but most importantly, I was wrong. This realization began to eat away at me. What had I been taught? What was it that I believed? And why? These questions fueled my desire for truth. I began really investing in my studies. I dug in. I began to question everything, but I also began finding answers. The right ones.

This whole time I was being enlightened, those around me were not. The ones I was serving with at my church were still in the same old place of thinking. They were happy there. I kept serving and kept loving those I served with. I now had the addition of not just serving those who came to the services, but I actually felt love toward them. I always wanted people to come to God, please don't misunderstand, but I had been indifferent about their choice to stay or leave. With this change of heart, I felt remorse if someone decided to attend elsewhere or return to their old life. I felt an emotional pain when someone would lose hope, feel loss, or be in pain, whether spiritual or physical. My life was changing. My mind was changing. I was changing.

I finished my studies and became a licensed minister when I was thirty-seven years old. I had found answers to questions I had had since I was a boy. I found answers I had just begun to ask the questions for. And I found questions that I didn't know I needed to be asking. I began to really dig in, and I was using the tools I had been taught in my studies. I now knew how to not only read but to understand the Scriptures. I had also been taught that it was ok to have questions. It was ok to ask them. Because without questions, there are no answers.

Not too long after I became licensed, I began to be emboldened to ask questions. I began asking questions of my friend even today and pastor at the time, who I'll call Andrew. I asked questions like, "Why do we believe that a person has to speak in tongues in order to know if they have received God's Spirit?" and "Why do I feel like something is missing when I baptize people?" The answers I would get were Scripture-based, and he had conviction about his answers. But my new understanding of these same Scriptures and having been taught to read the context of the Scriptures to bring out their intent was making it difficult for me to just take his word for it. I loved Andrew very much, but I could not go back to just taking a pastor's word for it. I could no longer just take anyone's word for it.

This caused me to have an intense feeling that something was missing. In fact, the feeling was so strong that it made me literally fear that I was going to have to answer to God for what I had been doing. The way I had been baptizing people was scripturally correct, but it felt empty. It felt like these souls who were getting baptized had no idea why they were doing it. When I looked into their eyes as I was baptizing them, I saw only emptiness. The wonder and joy of the realization of who God really is: that is what was missing. Trying hard not to be judgmental, I began to feel like some of these baptisms were happening more out of a desire to fill a necessary spiritual checkbox in order to not feel bad about what they had done in the past. I knew that feeling because I had it myself when I was baptized. All three times. At the time, even I had not come to the realization of how great God was and how loving He could be. The joy and wonder of who He is was not yet a part of who I was. My journey was only beginning, and I thought I had just arrived at the finish.

At the time, I felt as though I was learning, but I also felt that God had called me to do something. I did not know what that thing was. I was stressed out daily. Overworked. I had a family of five, including myself, and I was never home. My kids were addicted to video games and never left their rooms. My wife was stressed because no one was there to help her, and she was keeping it to herself. She saw that I was serving God with everything, and so was she. She was not going to step in the way of what God was doing in our lives. Besides, this change in me was exactly what she had been praying for.

The problem was that while I was hearing from God, I wasn't actually listening. As a new, inexperienced, and immature Christian, I had not yet come to the place in my walk where I knew what faith was. I had been in church my whole life, but I had never been taught, or given, the tools to actually live Christ-like. Sermon after sermon, I would be at every service, sometimes all day on Saturdays, and sometimes every night of the week. But still, I was not growing. So now an adult, a licensed minister, and a very curious Christian, I questioned everything. My questions were valid, but there were no new answers. I began to feel like I had when I was younger. Church was all smoke and no flame.

I needed more. People were leaving our church on a regular basis. New people would come in and stay for a while, and they too would leave. There was drama and finger pointing, and I just kept serving, and given the opportunity, I would work as a mediator between folks embroiled in the drama and do my best to impart God's wisdom so they could better decide how to handle their part of the drama and move on with God. I would pray with them, and they would leave feeling better. Most of the time, they would even solve their issue and come back and tell me they were glad they had asked me what to do because what I had told them worked. Other times, we would end the prayer, and they would do their own thing. Either way, I was just glad to have been given the opportunity to show them God's love. As my grandfather always told me, "You can lead a horse to water, but you can't make him drink."

In my last year of theology, the church split. Most of my closest friends left. It was a church of maybe three hundred people and more than twenty got up and walked out. Since I worked in the media and was there before everyone, couldn't leave the booth during service much, and usually was the one locking the doors, I didn't realize such a big problem was afoot. My good friends never really spoke of it to me, and that actually hurt. But I loved them all a lot. What hurt more was that, where I am from, people will stop talking to you altogether when you no longer go to their church. A silly and ignorant idea that I have hated most of my life. So many friendships, and lives, ruined because people feel the need to excommunicate themselves from those who leave their pews. They have not necessarily left God, just the building. But don't talk to them or devils are going to jump all over you and you will turn green and die. An exaggeration, of course, but you see how stupid it is. My friends were gone, and they quit talking to me. And because of a lifetime of church tradition, I did not talk to them either. It was not my pastor's fault that I did not talk to my own friends. It was my own. And I was ashamed of my decision. Not only that, my fledgling relationship with God was also weighing in on this, and God was not happy! Something needed to change. I needed to change.

After more than a year of no contact, I heard that the daughter of one of my closest friends had been assaulted and was in the hospital in pretty bad shape. I was crushed. My friend was going through this and I was not there to support and encourage him and his family. Why? The rule being employed by the doctrine of the church taken from Scripture was to remove those creating division in the congregation so that believers would not be troubled in their belief in God or swayed by a polluted gospel. It would also be used if a person refused to believe in the good news of Jesus. These people had already left the church, on their own; they were not causing division; they were not non-believers. They had left because they felt that they could no longer grow where they were. Now I am not ignorant or naive. I know that there were other reasons this giant group of people decided to all leave, but that was between them and God. The point is that this rule only loosely applied to them and mostly before the split had ever happened. What is past is past. Still believers, they were entitled to God's love and forgiveness. Both of which I was more than capable of showing.

After hearing the news of our friend's daughter, my wife and I stopped everything we were doing and drove straight to the hospital. When we got there, it was as if nothing had happened. I embraced my friend and asked if there was anything we could do to help them. We spent the next few weeks praying for them and with them. We showed them God's love, and by His grace, our friendship never missed a beat. And even though we did not go to the same church, we went places together, had dinners together, and did life together. Their daughter recovered, got married, and had a child of her own. God was there.

During this entire process, and according to our combined previous belief and current doctrine, I was doing nothing wrong. But it still felt like I was. I kept asking, why was this feeling that something was missing so strong? Was it just the enemy trying to cause me to stumble? My pastor, Andrew, was doing what he thought was right and what he felt God was leading him to do. The other members of the congregation seemed fine; why was I having such a struggle? Pastor Andrew must have seen it too and began to slowly remove ministerial responsibilities from me. The only ones I actually had left were performing the baptisms and leading my team in the media department. He had always done the pre-baptism counseling and was now performing the prayer over those being baptized, and then I would do the actual baptisms. Then one day, he began doing those as well. I was back in the media booth where I "belonged," and all was well with our world. But it wasn't.

Having grown up in a military family, I have an immense respect for the chain of command. Following orders and the structure that is naturally built into that chain are part of who I am. The men in my family were not necessarily strict with this idea, but it always fascinated me. And when I was going through hell in my home life as a kid, structure and the chain of command gave me something to cling to. It let me know who was in charge and what I needed to do to survive the battle ahead. This mentality has stuck with me even to today, although it has been strengthened and purified by God. It is this mentality that makes me a fierce ally and a devoted friend, colleague, and employee. If I am on your team, you can count on me to accomplish whatever task you have entrusted to me. It is this fact that makes me extremely loyal and trustworthy. It was also this mentality that made the next trial in my life so extremely difficult to get through.

Trial By Fire

Shortly after my last grandfather passed was when the dam broke and I sinned against my pastor and friend, Andrew. I had just turned thirty-nine and was having health issues at the time, I had an appointment for investigative procedures to be performed, and my last grandfather had passed the week after Christmas the year before. I was hurting, I was confused, and I needed a break. After service one day, I decided I would let Pastor Andrew know that I needed a break. I had a great team, and they could take over while I handled what I needed to take care of. It would be fine. That's what I thought. The state of mind I was in had grown an attitude. I had let that spirit invite more and ultimately allowed a spirit of offense to rest on me that did not belong. The problem was that I did not recognize it.

I started the conversation after service with the tale of my health issues, explaining that was why I needed a break. To my surprise, he disagreed. He did not disagree because he was being selfish, although at the time I definitely felt that way. Blind to his true intentions, I began to get upset. In hindsight, I know that, as a pastor, it becomes your job at times to save people from themselves. Especially someone who, in a leadership role, wants to "step away for a while." It was not my intention to disrespect Pastor Andrew that day, but I did. I let the words of the enemy feed on my pain and turn me against my friend. Our argument was heard by several folks, although thankfully most had already gone.

This unexpected behavior brought an otherwise fruitful and blessed time in our lives to an abrupt end. The details of this event are unnecessary, but needless to say, my family and I no longer attend services there. It is important to note that with God's leading I have since asked him for forgiveness, and we visit from time to time.

God had been trying to lead me to a new place. Had I just listened, this entire story would be written with a lot more joy. The lesson now learned, the blessing is the same. What I learned was that God knows me. God knows that I will never leave the place He has put me. I will never leave a friend. I will always serve those in my charge until my last breath. God knew that if I could not hear His urging to leave, He needed to do something drastic to get my attention. If we are unwilling to listen to God and learn from Him, then we leave Him no choice but to pry us out of our comfort zone. God knew that my loyalty was not going to be broken unless I had a reason to no longer be loyal. He had to break what I had built so that He could build something better. I had to have every support in my life removed so that I would have no choice but to lean on Him.

Odd, isn't it? Comfort zone is the term we attribute to a place where we are comfortable. A place where we feel safe to live our lives the way we have learned to do so and with the least amount of effort. Yet when that space becomes embroiled in health issues, stressful confrontations, and other harm, we refuse to give it up. We refuse to move to a new space. We are so used to that space that we expect everyone and everything else to leave so we can maintain our effortless existence. What we don't realize—what I didn't realize—is that when we do that, we end up pushing the important things out too, ultimately ending up alone and ashamed. While we are in desperate need of forgiveness, the road just gets darker and longer.

It was a painful lesson. Not only had I lost my last grandfather, an entire church full of friends, and someone I was looking to as a mentor, I was also losing my family. My wife was hurt, my kids were hurt, my mother was hurt, and those in my circle who were on the fence about God had now been pushed so far out and away from church that coming back did not seem likely. All of this pain because I had not been listening.

In the new place I find myself with God, He made it clear that in order to love Him with all my heart, mind, and soul, I cannot have unforgiveness in my life. Not for anyone. Including myself. A true walk with God must be pure. Unforgiveness breeds fear, hate, lust, and a plethora of other sins that cannot exist in the presence of God's pure light. Haven't you ever noticed that, like roaches when the light comes on, darkness also hides? Light and darkness cannot exist together. If I have darkness in me, I cannot exist in God's pure light. I found out over the years that have followed that it is necessary for me to clean my spiritual house. My physical home soon followed.

The upheaval in my life had hurt, but because the desire of my heart was to follow Christ and to be Christ-like, I was soon able to see why God had led me through such an intense flame. At the time, like when I was a child, all I saw was the storm. God was still teaching me focus. He was still showing me that I cannot see without His eyes, I cannot hear without His ears, and I cannot love without His heart. As you, the reader, may know, in the times of our greatest pain, it is almost impossible to see past it. For me, still being taught these lessons, it was no different. I reacted instead of responding, and it ended badly. I had disrespected my friend because I had let my pride, my confusion, and my lack of relationship with God get in the way.

Sure, I had gone to Bible school and gotten a license, learned to study the Bible, and began to operate in the area that I felt God was calling me to, but I was not actually using the tools I had searched for my whole life. God needed me to read my Bible, seek Him in prayer, and open myself up to His will for my life. The questions that I had been experiencing were His gentle invitation to spend time with Him. And I could have—should have—taken the time to do so. If I had, perhaps the lesson I needed to learn, and have learned, wouldn't have taken so long to learn. Maybe, just maybe, I could have done what God sent me to school to do, and He would have shown me what was missing, and I could have helped myself and my church move into God's next. But I did not move. I did not listen. I was too busy doing the other things that "God" had called me to do. My business was so busy I needed to focus on that during the day. In the evenings, I needed to do the things that "God" had called me to in my church, like setting up for services, changing stage designs, setting up the projection systems, attending practices, and saving the church money in any way I could.

This was not what God had in mind. He needed me to spend that time in prayer. He needed me to open His Word and study it so He could write it on my heart. He needed a relationship with me that I thought I already had. I was serving, I was sacrificing, I was spending so much time at the church that I had none left to spend with family. For eight years, I drove past my grandfather's house, literally right past the front of his house, on my way to the church nearly every day of the week. I only stopped a handful of times. I would give anything, knowing what I know now, to go back and sit on the couch with one of the smartest, most interesting men I ever knew and listen to the stories he had to tell. And maybe, just maybe, I could share the good news of Christ in a way that only I may have been able to do for him.

This is my fuel. This one realization powers my desire to know God with every ounce of my being, to share that knowledge with anyone who will listen, and to never again let someone I know and love pass before me without having heard the story of what God has done in my life. And even more, what He can do in theirs. Hopefully, you too can now see that God was there.

Thankfully, God was not done. My wife and I began visiting other churches. We had to go somewhere, or so we thought at the time. We needed to get reconnected, and we needed to do it soon. My family began asking me to use what I had learned to deliver sermons for them on Sundays, and I reluctantly agreed. I did not feel worthy of such a great responsibility, but I gave it everything I had. I began to read my Bible regularly, and I would listen to the audio Bible every night as I fell asleep. My wife hated it, and so I would fall asleep with headphones on. I did this for months, and things began to change. There was a shifting happening in my spirit. My attitude began to change, and I felt

God for probably the second time in my entire life since I was a child. My wife now listens with me. God is there.

My life was changing, and God was at the wheel. I began to feel a release and a calling to attend the church where our friends who had left our previous church had settled. This church was not a new one, and it had gone through many name changes and splits over the years, but I felt like God was saying I needed to be there. But before I committed my life and family to a new church, I would have to get confirmation. I was not going to just assume I had heard from God and put my family through the pain of yet another church move. So, we began to visit on Sundays. Some of our friends had been going there for a few years now, were friends with the pastors of the church, and were also serving in various roles in the church. It seemed like a good thing.

It was probably the third or fourth Sunday visit, and while my wife was uneasy, I was intrigued. This pastor was the first one that I could remember who did not preach from a place of fear or fire and brimstone. He didn't teach of the God who was waiting for you to mess up so He could punish you. No, this pastor actually seemed to be preaching from context and using the very same tools I had been taught in seminary. It was refreshing to see a congregation getting fed by Scripture in a way that properly used exegesis to define context of the past and intent of the Scripture and then combine that knowledge with personal experience to allow them to attach that scriptural intent to the context of their own lives, which is called hermeneutics. I was taking notes, trying to prove what I was feeling or prove I was wrong. Either way, I wanted a place where my family could learn the way I had.

On that visit, I went to the pastor and I told him that I had gone to seminary, and I appreciated the way he taught. I also told him that even though I had schooling, I still felt like there was something missing. The conversation progressed until I got up the nerve to just ask what I needed to ask, "Do you know of any material that I could read and/or study that might fill in the blanks?" To my surprise, since we really did not know each other yet, this man took me to his office and proceeded to take books from his own library and hand them to me. Five or six in total, and he said I should "start" there. I was blown away. Never had anyone, except my grandfather, given me a book to borrow, much less a practical stranger. I was moved on a spiritual level, and as I walked to my car, books in hand, I knew this was where I needed to be. This is where my family could grow, if they chose to. And after prayer and a talk with my wife, there we stayed.

The secret hidden in **Hebrews 11:1** would never have been found had I not had questions. It would have remained unanswered and hidden had I not been taught how to study, investigate, and understand the words that were written and why. There would have been no reason to even look. However, because I had opened my Bible, because I had that righteous indignation rise up inside of me, because I had taken a stand and said, "No one is going to sway me from God," I found myself with the tools to answer one of my oldest questions. I found myself itching to find the answer. And I would soon find myself with the time to look.

The journey was wrought with pain, loss, confusion, and suffering. But that was all my own doing, not God's. Sure, God led me to that trial, but I was the one who decided I knew better, and I could do this on my own. I was the one who, like a rebellious child, took the reins from the instructor before He had finished teaching me how to ride the horse. I was the cause of my own pain, not God. But God is faithful, even still. He stood by in dismay as I bungled the story of my life and riddled it with holes. I was the one who damaged friendships that God could have maintained and while still taking me where He needed me to go. I did that. And I was wrong.

Answers

Just before my life went sideways and just after seminary, I was about thirty-seven and I needed some time away after two years of grueling work, study, and serving at the church. When you are making your own way, it is grueling work. Hard work. But when God does it for you, there is grace. I had been choosing to do it myself, so grace was still a phone call away. Regardless, I needed some time to reflect, and so I volunteered to drive Pastor Andrew and the assistant pastor, Mike, to a meeting in Heber Springs, Arkansas. It was a more than eleven-hour trip, but it gave me time to have conversations and get to know them both on a different level.

I also knew that when we got there, I would have nothing to do but wait while they had their meetings. I knew I would have the perfect opportunity to study and do so in one of the most beautiful places I had ever been. The view from the hotel room was of Sugar Loaf, a popular hike in the area that, by choice, can end with a short rock climb. If you made that climb, it would result in a breathtaking view. Having made the choice to complete the climb on a previous trip, I can say it was well worth the effort. On this trip, I would have loved to do my studies from there. However, the view from the hotel room was most tranquil, and I did not have the extra time to make the hike and then climb, both there and back, before finally sitting down to study. The room would just have to do.

Sitting at the table in my room and staring out the window at Sugar Loaf, I opened my Bible and turned to **Hebrews 11:1**. I prayed for God to give me understanding and wisdom, and I started up my laptop. I connected it to the hotel internet and began bringing up the tools I would need to adequately study the verse. The first thing I did was compare the direct translations of the original Greek to what was actually translated in my Bible. For the most part, it was close. Aside from some minor deviation, mostly formatting, it was as it was translated. But I wasn't satisfied. For one, the NIV has translated the original Greek as "confidence." What? I really began to press in. I had to find the answer. So I began to check definitions of each of the original Greek words, one at a time. When I got to "confidence" (used in NIV) or "substance" (used in NKJV and others), I found that the Greek word "hupostasis" (*Strong's* G5287) had a few interesting translations.

While the word, as translated in *Strong's Concordance*, means steadiness, confidence, assurance, or guarantee, it also listed "a support." This piqued my curiosity. What kind of support? And so began a word study that I still use today. I went to the *NAS Exhaustive Concordance*. I did lexical research and others. The more I searched, the more I found and the more curious I became. I was enthralled. Addicted to what might be. The answer was my destination, and the vehicle did not matter. There was nothing I would not look at until my curiosity, the nagging question in my mind, had been answered. And it was.

I arrived at *Thayer's Greek Lexicon*, and there it was. The definition that would change everything.

"1. A setting or placing under; thing put under, substructure, foundation. 2. That which has foundation, is firm. A. that which has actual existence; a substance, real being." [1]

I couldn't believe it. In that moment, the nagging question, the fire in my mind, fizzled out. Had I found the answer? I went back and read the verse again with my new definition plugged in. It read, "Now faith is the 'foundation' of the things hoped for, the evidence of things unseen." Was this true? Did it match Scripture? Or had I sinned by changing what was written?

I kept going. With my new question, and maybe the most important one yet, I dug deeper. Does this new definition fit the context in which it was written? Yes, it did. Does this new definition agree with other Scriptures that discuss faith? Yes, it did! In fact, Jesus, when He spoke of our faith or taught in parables, said it was like a firm foundation (**see Matthew 7:24, 16:13-19; Luke 6:48**). There are more, so many more. In each one, the Scripture spoke of faith, and in each, it was described as a foundation, a solid rock. Could it be that simple? Is faith my desire and effort to build my hopes and dreams on my belief in God?

---

[1] Joseph H. Thayer, (*"STRONGS NT 5287: ὑπόστασις" Thayer's Greek English Lexicon of the New Testament*. (Joseph H. Thayer, Hendrickson Publishers Marketing, LLC, June 2019), pp. 644. See also, https://www.blueletterbible.org/lang/lexicon/lexicon.cfm?Strongs=G5287&t=NIV. Accessed 6 May 2021.)

The answer is up to you. For me, the answer is yes! Why? Because upon finding this answer, the nagging question in my heart, mind, and soul went away. It was replaced with something I now hold much more precious than gold or jewels or even wisdom. It was replaced with a desire to make God the foundation of my life. To build everything I am, hope to be, or hope to have on Him. All of my friendships, my marriage, my business, my finances, my very existence. It all now has to be built on the belief that God is alive, God does care, and He has called me by name! There is nothing else. I cannot take another step. Not one more breath. Anything I do next must start, and end, with God. He is my foundation, and He is my protection from the storms. He is the reason I write this book. He is the reason I wake up in the morning. He is the reason I love my wife. He is the reason I love my kids. He is the reason I work, the reason I play; He is the reason I serve my community, church, and family. He is all.

Everything that would follow from that moment would be ok. Even though I was still not where I needed to be. Even though I was not, and will never be, perfect. The one who is perfect was leading, and now I finally recognized it. I finally opened my eyes and saw Him. I finally believe. He will be faithful to heal.

Why? Faith!

Evidence

The second part of **Hebrews 11:1** is "evidence of things not seen." It wasn't until many years later that God revealed this answer to me. Many studies done. Many searches alone and with others. Until one day, I was asked to review some podcasts and make a video about how listening to those podcasts, and having them available on demand, had changed my life. Admittedly, it had been a while since I had listened to them, and though I had listened to them once before, I could not honestly remember which one or how it had changed my life. However, I had been feeling an urge to teach people how to hear God's voice, how to find His grace, and how to study the Bible and find the answers they seek to the questions I know they have. So I accepted the task. I began listening to these hour-plus-long podcasts, one at a time, and came to one from Mother's Day the year before. As I listened, I heard the pastor read this verse:

> For since the creation of the world God's invisible qualities—his eternal power and divine nature—have been clearly seen, being understood from what has been made, so that people are without excuse.
> **Romans 1:20 (NIV)**

When I heard it, that same feeling from when I had found the answer to "substance" once again filled my heart, mind, and soul. I went back and I re-read **Hebrews 11:1** again, plugging in the new information. It now read, "Now faith is the 'foundation' of the things hoped for, the evidence of 'God's eternal power and divine nature.'" And once again, I asked the questions, "Does it fit?" and "Have I sinned?" I prayed, and I asked God these questions. I asked Him again for understanding, knowledge, and wisdom. He responded with, "Why does it matter?"

Wait. What? Why does it matter? I began to explain to God all of the reasons why it matters that I know the "evidence of the things unseen." I expressed all of the importance I could muster to explain why my salvation and the salvation of those I lead would depend on me knowing the answer. He still just asked, "Why does it matter?" And then He added, "Isn't my grace sufficient for you?" This new question broke me. Of course His grace was sufficient for me; I was ignoring the one thing I had been given that I did not deserve. His grace. That grace was what allowed me forgiveness for all of the things I had done that made me unclean. His grace had allowed me to grind at my business, serve at my church, seek knowledge of His Word, all while ignoring my first calling to pastor my home. I had been so engaged in making God my foundation and serving Him with everything that I was that I had forsaken the most important and most valuable thing God had given me: my family.

The instant realization that everything I had been working for, and everything I had already been given, had somehow gotten out of order was devastating. I had been doing everything as unto God, but I forgot the most important thing. What had He called me to do? I had such a broken childhood, yet God gave me a loving and stable marriage. But my zeal for God kept me at the church and at Bible studies instead of home leading her, teaching her, sharing with her, and loving her.

I had no real stable father figures growing up, yet God gave me three boys, His grace, and a desire to be a better father than any I had ever seen. But I was too busy grinding my business and serving God at the church that I had no time to be the father God had called me to be. How could I have missed it by so much? How could I have been so blind? How was I ever going to fix it? Could I fix it?

Faith Simplified

God is not finished with me yet. By His grace, I will be made whole. With His forgiveness, love, and mercy, my calling will be fulfilled. I am still working on it, and He is still working on me. My calling is to let His words minister to me first, my wife second, my family third, followed by my friends, my church, and my community. Part of knowing God's will for your life requires a modest understanding of foundations. God pointed me at this requirement through **Hebrews 11:1**. I believe His expectation was that, knowing I needed a foundation, I would then build upon it. My problem was that I did not understand how to build anything that wasn't electronic, and my mind was too one track that I couldn't see around it. My understanding in Scripture to this point was introspective. Everything was always about how I could change because I cannot change anyone else. I cannot force others to change or to be more Christ-like. I have to be the change they need to see. I got stuck there. You don't have to.

The construction process is not part of my everyday life, but it is now a part of my general knowledge. Knowing how a foundation is built and at what point you can actually start building on it has helped me to translate the how and why of my Christian walk by faith and apply it to my everyday life. Allow me to try and explain.

As I understand it, the first step in building a firm foundation is to know the soil in which we plan to set our foundation. From a spiritual standpoint, we need to know ourselves and what we are capable of. If the soil is too soft, it has to be prepared with materials necessary to keep the soil underneath our new foundation from shifting and allowing it to crack. Our firm foundation needs to have a solid and pure base to be built on. It is up to us to prepare that ground.

For the purposes of this correlation, our faith needs to be built on something dependable. Something that will not give under the pressure or the weight of our everyday troubles. It needs to stand firm even when the worst storms come and pummel it with wind and rain. The Bible says that faith comes from the word of God (**see Romans 10:17**). Before we can receive it, however, we need to prepare for it. The soil of our heart, mind, and soul need to be prepared for faith by coming to terms with who we were, who we perceive ourselves to be, and at least an idea of who God has called us to be. Even if we're wrong.

We need to think hard about what we do and say and be intentional about it (**see Haggai 1:5-7**). We need to think about who we are, and who God has called us to be. Then we can combine that knowledge with forgiveness of ourselves and those who have wronged us and ask for forgiveness from those we may have wronged (**see Psalm 139:23-24; Mark 11:25**). God cannot hear our prayers if we hold unforgiveness in our hearts for others. Prepare the field for harvest, or in this case, prepare the place we are planning on setting our foundation.

This preparation allows us to clear the weeds, rocks, and debris of our lives from the soil we intend to pour the foundation of our brand-new life with God into. Without this step, our old selves will fight against what we are trying to build. This conflict between surfaces will cause cracks to form in our new foundation. With cracks formed, the weeds of our old life will grow up between the cracks and begin to break apart the foundation of our new lives.

But once we have prepared the ground for our new foundation, we are ready to receive the gift of faith that God has for us. Our new, God-given faith should then be given back to, and placed solely in, God. No one else. This gift to the believer from God is the one thing that gives us what could be thought of as the only requirement for us to be considered righteous before God. By giving us a measure of faith (**see Romans 12:3-8**), He is not only providing us with salvation, but He is also proving that it was He who saved us and not we ourselves (**see Ephesians 2:8-9**). Because of His grace and forgiveness and by His sacrifice, we are made righteous. And then, by grace, we are allowed into the presence of God, where we are given the gift of His Holy Spirit. This gift makes it impossible for any of us to say, "I did this," and that what "we did" somehow resulted in our own salvation or the salvation of others.

The fact remains that God's grace, love, and forgiveness made a way for us (our soil) to be purified in such a way that we now have a place for God's free gift of faith (our new foundation) to be poured into us. And with our new foundation poured, we can now "live by" and "build on" His gift of faith (**see Romans 1:1-17**). In the end, by giving our faith back to God, we are in a sense accepting His gift and honoring the requirement of action to use it. The understanding that I feel God has given me on this is that faith is the action you take with the belief you hold in God, and faith definitely requires action (**see James 2:20**).

When you find that moment where you truly believe; when your heart, your mind, and your soul all come into agreement that God is, was, and will be, your heart is filled with undeniable joy. I can describe it as knowing that God is, that He has called you by name, and that He has loved you since the beginning of everything. And you just "know" it. When you get to this place, you will find that this knowing is undeniable. It is so strong inside you that it literally brings you joy when you think about it. What is happening around you will not matter once your focus is on Him. Joy and peace will always replace fear and turmoil.

In fact, as I write this, that joy is welling up inside of me causing tears to flow down my face. The simple knowledge that God called me by name, forgave me, and is leading me on this journey to an eternity with Him is truly overwhelming. The man I was did not deserve the mercy God gave him, and the man I have become struggles to earn it. The only thing I know is that the effort is so very worth it. The feeling inside me is undeniable, and I desperately want each and every one who reads this to get to the place with God that I am now—and beyond. To feel what I feel and experience the knowledge of, and have a relationship with, the creator of everything. Faith, to me, is where your new life grows feet, and action becomes imperative.

Faith gives you purpose. It is a gift from God, one that He gives once you believe in your heart that He simply "is." It is the knowledge of the fact that what you ask for in His name, you will receive and the guarantee it will be done. It is a knowledge that, because of the foundation you are building on, it is His will that you seek every day of your new life in Him. And that because it is His will you now seek, everything you begin to ask for with your belief in Him is something He has already called you to and wants you to have. It is with this foundation of faith, and the desire it gives you to do His will, that you go out and pray for the sick and they are healed. You pray for blind eyes and they are opened. You begin to walk in the authority of the calling that God has for you, and you "know" it. You find yourself having a divine confidence in what you ask for and begin to "know" that you are going to be heard. You will purposefully seek it, and with passion. So let His light shine through you. Let His will be done through you. Because if not you, then who?

Here I am, Lord! Use me.

> And without faith it is impossible to please God, because anyone who comes to him must believe that he exists and that he rewards those who earnestly seek him.
> **Hebrews 11:6 (NIV)**

Chapter 4
LOVING GOD

"God is love" (**1 John 4:8**). The Bible, specifically Jesus, tells us that we are to love the Lord our God with all that we are (**see Matthew 22:34-40**). He states that this is the "greatest" commandment and that the second greatest is to love your neighbor as yourself. It is impossible to please God without faith, which is why faith comes before intimacy with God (**see Hebrews 11:6**). And we all know that a true relationship requires intimacy.

Now intimacy can be several different things. It can be physical, like between spouses. It can be emotional, like between spouses or friends. It can also be truthful, also between friends and spouses. It is important to define your relationship with God, just as it is important to define your relationship with a friend or even a spouse. If you do not define your roles, the level of trust you will share and the level of physical intimacy that your relationship will contain will be affected. When there are unknowns, the relationship is introduced to doubt. Doubt is an unknown variable with neither party knowing the boundaries of the relationship, and each doing their best not to disappoint the other, but both failing despite their best efforts. Defined boundaries are important in every relationship.

Assumed boundaries are poison to every relationship. Sure, these assumed boundaries will start out innocent enough. And, in the beginning, they will serve us well and keep both parties' interests protected. However, there will always come a point where these assumed boundaries will become threatened by one party or the other, and this will usually happen around the time that one party either increases or decreases the level of their intimacy in the relationship.

Communication

To avoid this inevitable rift, we communicate by telling the other party consistently how we feel and what we expect from them during our relationship with them. If either party fails to communicate their intentions and expectations, the relationship is strained, and both parties will lose out. This principle is the same for every relationship, whether you're buying a car or courting a bride. If we fail to learn and implement these valuable communication steps, everything we are trying to accomplish is placed in jeopardy. Knowing now that we must communicate in order to have a meaningful relationship, we can discuss the fledgling relationship we are cultivating with our creator.

Even while writing this, I am forced to re-evaluate my relationship with God. Every word, every thought, and every sentence requires deep and authentic introspection. I am not perfect. My walk with God has been wrought with failure, disappointment, and doubt. In my mind's eye, it appears to me as though I am, at times, trudging uphill in the wind and rain while holding an umbrella that is turned inside out and constantly being pulled backward at every gust of wind. I am soaking wet and freezing, barely able to see where my next step will be placed, and worrying about what I should do next if the rain doesn't stop. And then I realize I don't have to do anything. God has been in control the whole time, but I keep trying to be in control. My struggle with the creator of the universe over control of my life is the cause of all of my worries. I then realize that the reason it is so dark and cold is because I am going the wrong direction and have turned away from the light.

I am no longer facing God, but instead, I am pulling against Him. Instead of moving away from the storm, I am running toward it while God keeps tugging at me to turn around.

This is what I shared earlier with you about relationships. God has defined His role. He has communicated His expectations and intentions to us all. But in our pain and struggle, we forget. In addition, we cannot make up our minds as to what our intentions with God are and what our expectations should be. We aren't even sure what God is capable of, so we don't know what to ask for. We don't know what we should expect from God. Why? We simply don't believe in Him. We think we believe, but if we were to really and truly dig into our souls and ask the question of whether or not we believe, and only if we were not afraid to be honest with ourselves, the answer would be, "No, we do not believe."

It's not because we don't want to believe. We truly do. The problem we have is our doubt. We consume ourselves with our daily lives, our jobs, our finances, and our desires. We assume that our lives will only get better if we grind a path out for ourselves. That the only hope we have at being better, having more, and working less is to work, struggle, and fight our way to the top. We think these things because we have been taught that the only way to be happy is to have nice things. Bigger homes, nicer cars, the prettiest wife, well-behaved children, etc. The problem with this mentality is that these are all things that are desired, but not necessary for our happiness. The struggles we go through are placed there by us.

This is not to say that God does not want us to have nice things or even these specific things. The issue is not whether God wants you to be a pauper or a rich man. The issue is whether or not you are going to trust God to lead you to your blessing. The only way you can do that is through a relationship with Him. The only way we can have a true relationship with God is for us to finally decide that what we want is irrelevant to what God wants to give us, to decide that we need to define our roles in this new relationship, strap in, and enjoy the journey.

How can we have a relationship with anyone where they have defined their role, they have told us what they expect of us, and they have told us what they intend to do as their part of the relationship, but we don't respond in kind and instead just let them guess why we are in the relationship in the first place? They have no idea what our intentions are, and they don't know what we expect from them. I would have to venture out and say that a relationship like that would probably not make it more than a week, a month at best. You can't have and keep friends that way. You won't be able to find and keep a spouse that way, and you certainly cannot do business that way.

I remember the start of my relationship with my wife. We both knew what we wanted from each other, but we had no idea what to expect. Our intentions, at least in the beginning, were clear, but as we moved forward, things began to change. As time went on, conversations were required to inform each other of the current state of our relationship, where we each thought it was going, and what that meant both to ourselves and to each other. I have no doubt in my mind that, had we not had those talks, our relationship would have died long ago because of lack of communication.

As our relationship has grown, these same conversations have been necessary at several pivotal points in our lives. We discussed whether we wanted to continue seeing each other. Did we want to get married? Did we want to have kids? How many? Did we want to keep trying for a girl? Did we want to buy a dog? You get the picture. The point is that communication is vital to the longevity and health of any relationship. Our marriage would not have lasted twenty-plus years without the ability to have conversations that were at times difficult but always honest and heartfelt.

This is the same kind of relationship we need to have with God. This type of communication can only happen if we have been preparing ourselves for faith as discussed in chapters 2 and 3. We have to start there. Then we need to continue to make corrections to our thoughts, behaviors, and words daily. This is, in part, what the Bible is referring to when in **Romans 12:1-2** it says that we need to be transformed by the renewing of our minds. This renewal has to take place every day. We are constantly made unclean and impure by going out into the world and simply living our lives. How much more impurity will we be exposed to when we are used by God and go out into all the world and preach the good news of Jesus to the lost? Just as we take a bath on a regular basis to remove the filth and disease from our skin and to make ourselves presentable in our homes, in our relationships, and in public, we also need to be cleansed spiritually.

Think of it as a spiritual bath on a daily basis. We take into account where we have been and where we are going to go. Then we ask the questions, "Will we be a pure place for God's Spirit to dwell? Will our thoughts be pure and our hearts be free from lustful desires, and will the words that leave our lips be life giving?" If the answer cannot be an emphatic and resounding "Yes!" then we need to spend time in prayer and ask God to search us, change us, and use us. Occasionally in our relationship with God, we are going to have to ask Him to even break us so that we can humble ourselves before Him and be capable of being an example of His love in this world.

Have you thought about your life yet? Have you prepared the soil of your life for God's faith in such a way that your relationship with Him can begin? Is it possible for you to honestly look deep into your own soul and desires and say, "God, I intend to do your will. Search me, Lord, for things that are not of you and illuminate that dark corner of my mind and soul with your holy light. Open my eyes to it so that I might correct it. Change me, O God, and make me more like you. And, if I am not to a place where I can be used by you, then break me, O God, so that I may be remolded by your hands, having my mind made clean, my eyes open to your light, and my heart open to your love. Use me, Lord, for whatever your heart wills"? Are your intentions and expectations made known to God by your own lips? He knows the desires of your heart. He made you. You cannot lie to God, and He cannot lie to you. It is literally a match made in heaven. Are you ready for it?

God knows we are not perfect. He is not expecting you to be something you were never created to be. He is not sitting in heaven waiting for you to screw up so He can send down lightning bolts or swarms of locusts or turn you into salt. While God is all of the things He is described as in the whole of the Bible, for the believer, He has made a new covenant. In **Galatians 2**, Paul describes a disagreement he had with Peter in which Paul reminded Peter that even the most zealous Jews who kept all of God's laws were not made righteous in God's eyes. The only way to be made righteous has to be through faith. He supports this idea with the logical thought that if following God's laws was all we needed to do to be considered righteous by God, then Jesus died for nothing. The sacrifice of Jesus, a man who lived without sin, satisfied the requirement for a pure sacrifice before God because He gave His life willingly and died for the sins of others. Yes, you and I are included (**see 1 Corinthians 1:2**).

How can Jesus have died for my sins and yours? Because you were called by name and loved by God before the creation of the earth just like Isaiah prophesied to Jacob (**see Isaiah 43:1**). Paul writes in his letter to the Ephesian church in **Ephesians 1:4-5** that we were called to Him before the creation of the world. How can you be called unless He knows your name? The point is that God is love, and He loves you and me completely. *"For God so loved the world that He gave His only begotten Son, that whoever believes in Him should not perish but have everlasting life"* (**John 3:16 NKJV**). Our relationship with God is predicated on one simple principle. Belief. So I will ask again, Do you believe?

Trust

If you have been following along, the communication you have been intentionally developing with God is leading you to a place where your belief and your faith are beginning to work together. Your prayer life is now growing stronger than ever, and you are seeing things with a different perspective. If not, that's ok too. You can start working on your communication with God now, and He will be faithful to respond in kind to show you a better way—His way. At whichever point you decide to grow a relationship with Him, God is always ready to welcome you into that relationship. In fact, He longs for it.

That said, this place where your belief and faith are taking you is a place where you begin to trust in God. Trusting God is not exactly like when you trust anyone else. If I loan a friend money and trust that he will pay me back, that has nowhere near the same return as when I trust that God's promises are true. My friend could be going through tough times, he could be a really good liar, or he just didn't remember he borrowed money from me. However, when God says He is going to do something, He will never disappoint. His promises are "yes" and "amen" as the Scripture says, and it is impossible for God to lie (**see 2 Corinthians 1:20; Hebrews 6:18**).

I remember so many times when I trusted so deeply in friends, family, and even pastors only to be disappointed. Not necessarily because they lied or were unwilling to honor their promises, but because life made it so very difficult for them to do so. When we, who are not divine, make promises to others, keeping those promises can be quite difficult. It isn't just that we don't want to, although sometimes that may be exactly the reason why; sometimes we simply cannot do it at the time it is required of us without sacrifice on our part. God will never withhold His promises regardless of the sacrifice required on His part. If you think this is not true, look at Christ Jesus, the only son of God, sacrificed for the sins of those who were not even born yet so that we might be forgiven and have the opportunity to have His spirit, just as He had promised in Scripture (**see Hebrews 10:17, 8:12; Jeremiah 31:34; Romans 5:8**).

What kind of father would allow His only child to die to save others who have rejected Him? What kind of son, knowing this was going to happen, would allow Himself to be taken, beaten, and tortured to death for things He is innocent of, just for the sake of being obedient to His Father? I have often sat and thought about what I would do if I were the son in that conversation: "Son, I know you haven't done anything wrong, but I need you to allow yourself to be arrested, taken to the torture chamber, and then hung until you die while naked and publicly shamed."

I think to myself what my answer would be, knowing what obedience to my father would mean for me. I have been obedient to everything my father has told me to do up to this point. I have been obedient to the law of the land and respectful of the wishes of others, even when they were rude about it. There were a few times when I corrected others, sometimes with fervor, but always with love. I see myself questioning the decision. I see myself fighting to preserve my own life. Justifying my argument with the just life I have lived and how I have done nothing wrong. But Jesus did not think this way. His example to us is that we lay down our lives for the sake of others. That if we can save even one life by giving ours, it is worth the cost.

How do we then justify our lack of belief? How do we live every day experiencing the benefit of who God is and what He has done without taking into account the sacrifices He has made to give that opportunity to us? Can we look at the whole of creation and seriously, with a straight face, say it was all an accident? Whether you subscribe to theories of the Big Bang or evolution, can you really deny that something or someone created it all?

In the case of Christianity, I look at all there is in the universe and I see the fingerprints of God. I do not deny that a Big Bang happened: the Bible says, "God said, 'Let there be light,' and there was light" **(Genesis 1:3 NIV)**. My book isn't meant to be a debate for or against evolution. As mentioned in a previous chapter, I do believe in microevolution, and I do believe that science has confirmed that we possess many similarities with many other of God's creations. Most of them are cute. Some of them are very strong. I would love to be cute and strong, but God only blessed me with one of those traits.

God does not need proof to exist, but He provides it in everything we see so that we may believe in Him. That is the kind of Father who is less concerned with what He wants for Himself and more concerned with what He can do for His children. That is a Father who, regardless of personal loss or gain, is more concerned with what His children want and need. If we can believe in Him, He is faithful to provide us with the faith required to please Him and to bless our efforts along the way. God is not out to get us. He is not a God who is looking for a reason to punish us. He is a God who wants every chance to spend time with us, the chance to teach us more about Himself and, more importantly, how to live a righteous life so that we can one day be forever in His presence.

Submit

He works in our lives to develop trust. He communicates with us in ways we will understand, even if it hurts. He is clear in His messages, but our own judgment, selfishness, and fears get in the way of what He is saying. When this happens, the message seems like He is trying to hurt us. If we would just back up and listen, we would see His plan more clearly. He is never out to cause a righteous man or woman pain. His ways are to prosper us and to give us hope (**see Jeremiah 29:11**).

Scripture reminds us that He wants to spend time with us and that, when we do, He will show us His ways and how they are meant to provide peace and joy in our lives (**see Revelation 3:20**). When Jesus was in the garden praying and He asked God, if it be possible, to let the cup pass from Him, He was asking His Father if He really had to do this. Being in a physical body meant that the divine creature inside would have to endure the pain and suffering of the cross. Even the divine being that Jesus was did not want to have to go through that suffering.

Doesn't that put the experience in perspective for us? He did it anyway. He said if His Father wanted Him to do it, He would. He submitted to the will of His Father. He loved His Father with everything He was. He trusted Him just as much. He knew that if He obeyed His Father, though the path was going to be torture, that His Father's promise of joy, peace, and glory forever was on the other side of that pain. Jesus knew that the pain was only for a moment and that His Father could not lie. Scripture says, "For the joy set before him he endured the cross, scorning its shame, and sat down at the right hand of the throne of God" (**Hebrews 12:2 NIV**). Jesus submitted to the Father all that He was, even His life. This is not an easy thing for anyone to do. I struggle with it. Do you?

Our lives are busy. We fill our time with all kinds of things that may, or may not, be important. While we are scheduling parties, meetings, and other things, we tend to forget that the time we have on this earth is finite. That means we only have a very specific amount of time here. And the worst part about that is that we don't know how much we have.

Even still, we spend it like water. We go places and do things that have no real meaning. What if we stopped, focused our lives, and started using our time like currency? We would realize that it is more valuable than all of the gold on the planet. Then we'd spend it with purpose, giving it to the ones we love, and those who love us, those who need us, and those who need God, instead of wasting it on the pursuit of money, working endless hours for people who may not really care about us, or spending too much time watching TV and movies made by people we don't even know and who most likely do not care about us except for the cash we might put in their pockets. Why do we do these things with something so precious? Are there not better things we could be doing with our time, more precious people we could be spending time with? And, because we are then using our time as currency, can we not give some of it back to the one from whom it comes?

I struggle with this every day. I question what I spend my time on. How do I spend it? Why can I not spend more time with God? What is stopping me? Who can I spend time with instead of my TV? Where could I take my family instead of the couch? These are all real questions that I ask myself every day. And, honestly, I still have not solved most of them. I have spent so many years living life the wrong way that even now, nearly a decade into trying to live it right by God, I still have these issues. Why? Because I created a mess with the decisions I have made up to this point, and with God's help, I will make new choices, wiser choices, that will lead me to the life I want to live. His will in my life is now the desire of my heart, and everything I do is meant to glorify Him, to bring honor to Him. Every word I say, every place I go, everything I choose to be a part of: all are passed through one filter. Do they bring honor and glory to God? If not, I don't do them.

This is not easy, but the more you practice it, the easier it becomes. The choices I make today are not the same as the ones I made in my youth. But God is faithful. The things I have jumbled up and messed up in my life are beginning to unravel. My wife, kids, family, and friends are beginning to see God through me. My neighbors are coming to know God through me, and I am so very grateful. The sacrifices I make on a daily basis are counted as joy because of God. The blessing of that joy is all because I have decided to submit my life, mind, and tongue to God. And it is so very worth it.

Born Again

Learning to communicate with, trust in, and submit to God are very important steps on the way to being Christ-like. I tell the men in my ministry that if Jesus did it, said it, or thought it important enough to mention, then who are we to act, speak, or think differently? We are not gods. We have no divine purpose or thought without God. So how can we overrule Him? Jesus had to pray, Jesus had to read the Scriptures, Jesus had to obey God, Jesus had to submit to the law of His land and time, so who are we that we might know better and do differently? If it was required for Jesus, then it should be only the start of the depths we should go to submit to our Father, who has adopted us by grace through mercy.

When we accept and understand that we can do nothing without God, we begin to realize just who we are. Through the sacrifice of Jesus, the sacrifice required by the law has been satisfied for all of us who believe. Because of that, when we believe in Him, our sins are forgiven. In that moment, we are offered the chance to become children of God. When we accept, He then grants us a measure of faith. With that faith, we begin a new relationship with our heavenly Father. One in which we are born again by His Spirit. And, by His Spirit we are made new. The old version of us has been washed away, and the new version is standing righteous before God. It is then up to us whether we honor Him with our lives or remain selfish in the flesh.

However, when we choose to lay down the things that were causing us to fall short of the glory of God, when we decide—like Jesus did—that what God has for us is worth the sacrifice required to acquire it, that is when we find that our lives are changed. We are no longer living for ourselves, but giving all that we are to Him, and He is using it to reach others. We then begin to see that it is not just our lives that have changed, but the lives of those around us are also changing. Those whose lives seemed to be lost are now seeing God through our words and actions, and they begin to see the path to a better life.

When your neighbor, who only knew the person who cussed, got drunk frequently, partied hard, was broke all the time, and/or perhaps had a drug use problem, sees that person begin to no longer do those things, they notice. You may think, like I once did, that the things you do and say are irrelevant and that no one really cares what you do because it only affects you, but you're wrong. There are people in your circle of influence right now who are watching you. They either want to be like you, or they would like to see you make better choices. Either way, when God enters your life and you become a new person in Christ, those who are watching you receive joy. Their lives are changed because they saw yours change. They can then glorify God for the work He has done in your life and theirs.

I thank God every day for the change He made in my life. That change has been noticed by every member of my family; it has sparked change in some of their lives and curiosity in all. I have seen people I knew before come and tell me they want to know what happened to me because they want what I have. In the last decade alone, I have had people who I was ministering to in the beginning of my walk with God come to me with tears and tell me that their lives are now forever changed because of the love of Christ that I poured out on them. I only poured out that love because of who God had made me to be. I genuinely saw a person who needed God in their lives, and I did not want to see another person fall short and lose their life because God wasn't in it. We all know people like this. You can reach them through Christ. You can be what they need if you are willing to lay down your life for Christ and love them through their hell. You might get burned, but God is faithful to restore anything the enemy tries to take from you.

The point is that if you love God with all of your heart, mind, and strength, He will create in you a right spirit. He will make His will the desire of your heart, and He will walk with you through the fire. You will do what He has called you to do, and you will find joy in suffering for Christ. If we want to enjoy the glory of God that Jesus enjoys, we must also be willing to endure the suffering that Jesus endured. We cannot enjoy the reward without the sacrifice. No gain without the pain. This does not mean that your life with Christ will be riddled with suffering. On the contrary. While my life can have moments of turmoil, loss, and pain, there are more times of blessing and favor than not. I experience God's grace more than the enemy's sword. God is faithful, and I trust Him with everything I am. The measure of faith He has given me I have placed completely in Him and nowhere else. He leads, He speaks, He changes everything. All I do is put one foot in front of the other as He tells me where to go.

Purpose

Now that God has created in me a new man, I can walk without shame or condemnation for the things of my past. I have asked for and received forgiveness for the things I have been guilty of, and Jesus paid the price. My goal from that point on has been to honor that sacrifice. Who can I share the good news of Jesus with? Who needs God's love in their life? How can I be used by God to fulfill that purpose?

These questions are just a few of the thoughts that run through my mind as I live intentionally, every day, with the purpose of honoring God. These thoughts create an environment where I desire to die to self every day and spend time speaking to God. It is important to note that spending time intentionally seeking God on a daily basis creates a desire inside me to seek His will for my day. The foundation that is my faith only intensifies this in everything I do throughout the day. My prayer time is built on it. The business or work I perform during the day is built on it. Everything I do and think is filtered through, and built on, my faith.

This leads me naturally to a place with God where I have sought for, approached, and spoken to Him before I ever left my house. Every day! What I have found is that by doing this, my days become fuller. I have more joy, despite what may come. Because I am praying to Him throughout the day, I can ask Him to heal, bless, and forgive not just myself, but anyone I encounter who may need it. We are instructed by Scripture to pray without ceasing, and when we do, we never leave God's presence. This behavior makes it so much easier to truly love the Lord our God with all of our heart, mind, and strength. And, because it is something we are training our hearts and minds to do, there is a promise of blessing that comes with it: the blessing of God's attention.

The more time I spend with God, the more I find that I naturally begin to wonder what God thinks of what I am doing, saying, eating, drinking, and participating in. I no longer worry about what others might think of it. God's opinion matters more every day that I am alive. This has changed the way I think, the way I act, and even how I interact with people I have known for years. The key is that the more I love God, the more I love those around me. In fact, God seems to grant me a higher capacity to love. Offense is so rare it will soon be a thing of the past for me. I find myself desiring to pray for people. I want to listen to their problems, pray for them, and then listen to God as He speaks to them and gives them wisdom in their trials. I want to walk beside a man who is struggling and be God's light on the path.

I want to show God's love and be used by God to open the eyes of others to the possibilities through Him.

When we position ourselves to be used by God, He draws us closer to Him. His power will work through us, and His voice can be heard in our words and actions. This happened to Paul, Daniel, Abraham, and many others. My favorite is the story of the three Hebrew boys Meshach, Shadrach, and Abednego. Their real names were Hananiah, Mishael, and Azariah, but they were changed when they were taken to Babylon after the fall of Jerusalem. Most of us, if not all, know the story as it is told. These three young men were from the royal household in Jerusalem, and they were chosen, with the help of Daniel, to be placed in the position of administrators for the king of Babylon's household. The king of Babylon at this time was Nebuchadnezzar. I recommend you read the book of Daniel and see what I am talking about.

The reason this story is so amazing to me is because these three young men, being from the Jerusalem royal family, would have been looked upon as leaders by those of lesser standing from Jerusalem and also by their peers. This is interesting because when the king made his proclamation and these three would not bow to his statue, they did not dishonor the king, who had been taking great care of them. They respectfully declined his commands.

Remember when you were a kid and your parents told you to do something. They would give you the consequences of not doing what they said. Something like, "If you do not clean your room, I am going to beat the devil out of you!" Your parents may not have been the corporal punishment types, but hopefully you get the idea. These boys had been told that anyone who did not bow down before the king's statue would be thrown into a fire and burned alive. Basically, "Do it! Or die!"

Up to this point, these three had been living peacefully in the king's household. They were performing the duties with which they had been tasked in such a way that the king actually grew to admire them.

They were intelligent, good looking, and hard working. I imagine that everything they did for the king of Babylon, they did as though it was for God. I know I would.

At the time of the decree from the king, these guys were on good terms with him, they were living better than most of the other captives from Jerusalem, and they had the ear of the king. Because of their faithfulness to God and their obedience to His Word and commands, God had kept His promise from the Scriptures and gave them favor with both Himself and the king. God blessed them with authority in a land where they did not belong. He made even their enemies to be at peace with them.

On the day of the decree, I imagine the scene as one where the king on his throne is seated in a higher elevation from the general audience so all could see and hear. I imagine that these three boys are up on the platform with the king and that they are in plain sight of the crowd, which included the rest of the captives from Jerusalem. I see the command being decreed, and I see the sea of people before them all bow down to the king's golden image, except for these three. The king, obviously shocked, commands them one last time to bow, but when they respectfully but expressly decline, citing that it was a sin against their God, he gets very upset. I can hear the king then loudly demand that these three bow or be thrown into the fire. I can see the fire perhaps just to the side of this platform. A raging inferno. High enough off the ground so that those in the back could see and with either open sides or windows. Punishment of the people would only work if they could all see the consequence firsthand, so this would be a very public thing.

The Scripture tells us that when these three refused the king's command the second time, the king ordered the fire to be made seven times hotter than it ever had been before as a show of force (**see Daniel 3:19**).

At this point, and with the attention of every person in attendance now on the platform, I see the king becoming offended to the point of rage that these three who he has taken care of and provided for are being so insolent. They're refusing to obey despite his kindness up to this point. I can see the distorted look on his face as he seethes anger. I can feel the emotion coming from him as if it were my own. He looks out on the crowd; a hush has fallen over them as they await the king's response. Most who are citizens probably already know what is about to happen as a murmur begins to be heard throughout the crowd. I can almost hear the thoughts of the king as he thinks to himself, "Why are these three so eager to die?" Then I hear the conflict inside his mind. He really likes these three; their work has profited his kingdom. But if he does not follow through with the punishment, he will lose control of his people and rumors will spread that he is weak. This will lead to other kingdoms planning attacks thinking the king an easy target. He cannot have this. It would ruin him. He must act! His hand now forced, and the anger brewed almost as hot as the fire, he yells at the guards to bind their hands and feet tightly and throw them into the fire. With the crowd now staring in awe of these three who have defied the king, the king acts swiftly and violently.

"Throw these three insolent fools into the fire!" I hear him exclaim. "Let any in this kingdom know that I am the most high king, and any who would refuse me WILL BURN!" I hear a hush come over the crowd, quickly followed by sounds of friends and family beginning to mourn. Perhaps a handful of believers begin to pray. Some ask God why He would allow this. Maybe they begin to wail as they lose hope all together. Perhaps the people of Jerusalem have been captive for so long they have given up hope and lost their faith because their circumstances feel insurmountable. Bigger than God even.

As the guards grab these three and bind them with ropes so that they cannot somehow escape the fire, the crowd is a mixture of cheers for the power of the king and wails of terror at the thought of what will come next for those from Jerusalem. Terrified, confused, and full of doubt, these once-proud people stand mixed into a sea of faces they do not recognize, in a place that is not their own. Some have endured indescribable indignities. Their hearts drop into their stomachs as the guards pick up these three bound young men and hurl them into the fire from the platform. What happens next sends shivers down my spine.

Each of the guards commanded to throw these young men into the fire is killed as they carry out their orders. I can hear their screams of pain as they fall to the ground dead from the heat of the fire. I can hear the thud as the three young men hit the ground inside the fire, perhaps landing on hot coals and burning logs. I hear the logs begin to shift and fall from the stack as each of these three land on or near them and roll off. I see the sparks from the stoking of these coals swirl up into the sky. But there is something missing. I should be hearing screams of pain and terror, but I am not. I look out into the terrorized crowd, and I see once tearful and contorted faces beginning to look up in curiosity. They too are wondering why there are no screams or sounds of any kind coming from the fire. When the guards had died from the flames, they had screamed for more than a minute before falling silent, but these three haven't even made a sound. The crowd's puzzled looks of inquiry as they struggle to peer over those standing between them and the fire begin to turn to amazement. The people of Jerusalem slowly begin to see what has happened, and those from Jerusalem in the crowd slowly begin to stand while their wailing turns to cheers.

In wonder at what these people have begun to cheer for, the king begins to peer over the side of the platform with the remaining guards and staff. Just then, I see what he sees, and my spirit is overwhelmed with joy. I don't know how, but I know what I see is an angel sent from God standing in the midst of the fire walking and having conversation with the three who were thrown in. How? The king is dumbfounded. Bewildered, he asks the staff, "Didn't we throw just three men into the fire?"

Equally confused, the staff reply, "Yes, your majesty. There were only three." The reaction of crowd, now in awe, has grown to a mixture of cheering and bewilderment. The king stares into the fire for a few minutes, trying to wrap his mind around what he is seeing. Soon he orders the guards to fish these men out of the fire. I see the first two pulled out without a scratch on them. As the guards pull the third to safety, the fourth man simply disappears without a trace. I watch as each of those on the platform begin to inspect these three. Their bonds have been removed by the fire, but they and their clothing are untouched. They don't even smell like smoke.

The crowd, now silenced to a hush, are all standing. Every last one of them are eagerly waiting to see what happens next. For the people of Jerusalem, I can see from the looks on their faces that their faith has been restored. Their hope has returned, and the feeling that God has forsaken them has gone. Every one of them, including a great number of the king's own people, have seen the God of Israel move. Some don't know what they just saw and are looking for someone to provide answers. They are beginning to converse with those from Jerusalem and to ask questions. The people of Jerusalem begin to provide answers.

These three young men found purpose. The belief they had in God had given them the desire to honor Him with their lives and their actions. Their faith in God gave them strength and a desire to do God's will no matter the cost. Their devotion to that belief, through the actions of their faith, led them to a fruitful prayer life with God. They remained devoted to God despite their circumstances. They would not give up hope that He would save them because they had been speaking to Him on a regular basis. They loved God with everything they had, including their own lives. They held nothing back, and they proved their love for God to the entire nation of Babylon that day. So much so that the king even changed his decree.

Oh, how easy it really must be to endure trial by fire. Especially when you have a personal and loving relationship with the God of all creation. With a relationship like they had, your perspective changes. You begin to see the world through God's eyes. You begin to love in ways you never thought possible. The image of yourself that you see in the mirror begins to change as God shows you your purpose. He begins to show you what He really thinks of you. He illuminates the dark places of your life so that you can clean up who you think you are and make yourself more like Jesus. He wants to have a relationship with you so much that He gives you grace and forgiveness while you do.

With your past forgiven, your present filled with God's love, and your future now defined by God's Holy Spirit, you're ready to walk through fire and even on water. Because it's all about whether or not you can see from God's perspective. A relationship with God like the one these three had will give you the ability to see from a divine point of view. When it does, there is no longer anything to fear, there is no longer any shame, and you will realize the blessed purpose that God has called you to.

Love God with every part of your being. Honor Him with your words, your actions, and your life. Let Him use you. Hold nothing back. Keep nothing hidden. Let Him embrace you and tell you that you are His own.

Chapter 5
LOVING YOU

Probably the most difficult thing in this world to do, for most of us, is to love ourselves. For one reason or another, there seems to always be something about us that we dislike. Our hair is too straight or too curly; we're too thin; we have too many freckles or too many wrinkles, etc. For whatever reason, the mirror we stand in front of seems to highlight every imperfection we have. And we are all too eager to pick them up and dwell on them.

Even when others come to us and compliment us on our better qualities, we deny what they claim to see. We hold on to the image of ourselves that we believe to be true, latch onto it with both hands, and grip it tight as if it were gold. Why? If we dislike that part of ourselves so much, why not let it go? Why not enjoy the compliments? Why not?

I believe the reason for this is our inherent tendency to cling to negativity. We can have 364 days of bliss and beauty. Have everything we try go right. But when day 365 goes south, we have somehow had the worst year of our lives. Why? I feel like God asks the same question. I believe He says, "I have given you all that you need to succeed. I have made you in my own image. I have blessed you, walked with you, and held you when you could not go on. Why do your eyes only see what you do not have?"

When God laid this on my heart, I was immediately made aware of how I too was looking at the world. You read earlier about portions of my life. In each portion, I stated that God was there. Let me tell you how I know. Because He will never leave me or forsake me.

Keep your lives free from the love of money and be content with what you have, because God has said,

> **"Never will I leave you; never will I forsake you."**
> **Hebrews 13:5 (NIV), emphasis added**

This simple verse tells me that if I keep my focus on Him, if I intentionally line myself up with God, if I remember that in all things God is there, then I will be content. I will have peace in my struggle. I will have help in the midst of the fire.

Storms

How do I know this from one verse? Because I have put it to the test. I have stood in my struggles and looked around. I stood in my storm, and I felt the wind trying to push me down. I felt it trying to push me off course. I stood in the midst of the sea of my struggles, and I saw the waves. I felt them crashing over me trying to crush me with the weight of everything I was powerless to control. And then I saw God. In the moment that I saw God, there was peace. The wind, the waves, and even the fire were unable to harm me because they were made by God. God created them, just like He created me.

If I truly believe that, then the wind and the waves only have power that God provides, just like me. I am a creation of the most high, but because I believe and God has given me faith, I am made different. I have been adopted by God and made one of His children. Chosen by God, I now have power from the Father. Just as a child adopted by the king would have power through the crown of their father, I too am granted power through the crown of my Father.

When the storms of our lives arrive, we need the perspective to see God. We need to be able to walk over the top of the storm. If you're anything like me, you will have, at one point in your life, thought that if you plan everything out just right, talk to people a certain way, avoid certain people, avoid certain areas and events, then everything will be ok. Somehow if you can juggle all of these things and do just the right things at just the right times, you will avoid the storms altogether. Wrong!

I tried this for a very long time. I studied the way people spoke. I studied their body language. I even studied psychology thinking that if I just learn how to spot behavior markers ahead of time, I won't have to deal with the drama or the violence of this world. But no matter how hard I tried, I could not avoid the storms. I kept finding myself in one dramatic situation after another. Without exceptions, every situation, every relationship, every choice would eventually lead me to a storm. Then it occurred to me. The problem wasn't that my choices, actions, and words were leading me to storms. Everything I had control over was being considered. I was micromanaging nearly every aspect of my existence, and I was miserable because it was exhausting, and it wasn't working. The problem was the choices I had no control over—other people's choices.

No matter how hard you try, no matter how right you are, no matter how perfect the scenario, the intentions, or the planning: none of us can control the choices of another person. Meaning I cannot control the choices of any other person in all of creation except my own. Sure, we can influence the decisions of others. Through pressure or even force, you can make another person do, and even say, the things you want them to. But what would you have really accomplished in the long run? They still do not agree with you, and they will at some point get the opportunity to change what you have made them do. So really, why try?

Storms are not always bad. However, whatever they are, once you have the relationship with Him that places you in His presence perpetually, you will no longer experience the storm in the same way. Take Peter, for example. Jesus, seemingly on purpose, led him into a storm in **Matthew 14**. Once there, though, Jesus did not leave him in his storm. And God will never leave us in ours.

With his belief firmly creating a path where he could honor God with his life, his words, and his actions, Peter found himself in a relationship with God that perhaps he was unaware that he had, experiencing things in his lifetime that until then had been only talked about in stories. Perhaps as a child, he learned some of these things about God, but until this moment, he had never really contemplated the extent to which he was willing to go to truly trust God. In this moment, he fully embraced the idea that God was there, and maybe, just maybe, this Jesus fellow really and truly was the Son of God.

In that moment, at the height of a storm that would have drowned them all, Peter stood up in the tiny boat as he sees what he perceives to be the outline of a man walking toward them. But how? They were in the middle of a large body of water. It was not possible for a man to be out there, but he saw no other boat. Could it really be? He believed that the man he saw through the wind and rain, walking on water, was in fact Jesus, whom they had left on the shore earlier.

Can you imagine being in the boat with Peter and seeing a man walk out to meet you? Would you be scared? Or would you be as Peter was, excited to see him? Personally, if I did not have the relationship with God that I have now, I don't think I would be all that excited to see a man walking on the water in the middle of what could be described as a hurricane. It would genuinely freak me out. I would see this guy out there walking on water, and I would be intrigued. My mind would be trying to figure out what was going on. Trying to figure out how this trick was being pulled off. However, I would be totally freaked out. I would be so uneasy, and I certainly don't think I would step out of a perfectly good boat into the waves of a raging storm because whatever this was had asked me to!

Now, in this same scenario, if I had a relationship with the one walking out on the water, if that relationship was a bond made over a strong belief in God, and I was in the place I am today in that relationship with God through lots of prayer and fasting, as we are called to do, I would not have hesitated even for a second to leap from the boat and run on the water to meet Him. The difference being that in my intentional relationship with God, I would have been given faith to accompany my belief; like Paul and Jesus have said, all things are possible when we believe.

Peter stepped out of the boat, and he did walk on the water. But, like we all tend to do, he began to focus on what he did not have control over. When he changed his focus, the only things he could see were the wind and the waves. Not a good thing to dwell on when you're in a hurricane.

Our lives can sometimes be a hurricane. In the midst of that hurricane, we need to keep our focus on God. If we can, He will give us the strength to rise above the wind and the waves, and we will then be able to go through the storm, but not have to endure the storm.

The Mirror

The wind and waves recognize the voice of their creator, and so do we. Oftentimes, we tend to turn from that voice in an attempt to justify our choices. Doing so only makes things worse, and we end up coming full circle right back to the place where we have to make a decision or obey God's voice. Can you imagine what it would look like if the wind and waves tried to do their own thing instead of being still when Jesus told them to? I am grateful that I am created in the image of God. That every part of who I am knows the voice of God. That even my dead, dry bones will respond to the sound of His voice. Just like the wind and the waves. But unlike the wind and waves, God gave us free will, the ability and privilege to choose which path we are going to take: His or our own.

When we come to know God the way He intended, when we are walking side by side with Him—sometimes hand in hand, and other times being carried in His warm embrace—and when we find ourselves in His perpetual presence like this, He speaks into our lives, He heals us, He blesses us, He corrects us, but most of all, He loves us. I believe that this comes naturally to Him and that God's divine nature is love. When we begin to see ourselves in God's mirror, we also begin to see ourselves in the image of God. We begin to speak into our own lives, we begin to heal ourselves spiritually and emotionally, we begin to bless ourselves and allow ourselves to be blessed, we begin to correct ourselves and allow ourselves to be corrected, and we begin to love ourselves and allow ourselves to be loved. Through this process, we also do one important thing: forgive ourselves.

When we realize, and accept, that we are made in His image and have been made His children, then we begin to do something amazing. We finally begin to know who we are, what our purpose is, and why God has chosen to love and forgive us the way He has. We see in His mirror an imperfect and weak creation that is made perfect in Him. The gift of faith that was granted simply because we chose to believe in Him has now planted a seed in our hearts, a seed of love and forgiveness that has no choice but to bear fruit.

As a creation of God endowed with free will, we, unlike most of the rest of creation, have the choice of denying this seed the opportunity to grow. Just like any other seed, it needs light, it needs to be fed, and it needs fertile ground to prosper in. If we choose to return to the life God has freed us from and if we choose to harbor unforgiveness for ourselves and others in our hearts, this new seed begins to be choked out by the weeds of our humanity. If left unchecked, these weeds will begin to grow out of control as we move further away from God's light, and eventually the new thing God has planted will die. This is why it is extremely important that we remain in front of God's mirror as much as possible. Perpetually.

God's mirror is the place between us and God, in front of which we stand in order to inspect ourselves for imperfections. We search intentionally for the things in our lives that are not of God, the things that do not honor His sacrifice, and the things that do not bring glory to His name. This mirror is created by our belief that He exists. It is polished by the gift of faith that He has blessed us with, and it is lit by His Holy Spirit. As long as we stand before this mirror, there will be nothing new that can enter our lives that does not bring life. In front of this mirror, things of our past that have brought death, shame, and pain into our lives are illuminated, and we are made aware of their presence.

The shame and sin of our past is quick to punish us. Because of this, we will often develop a defense mechanism that allows us to ignore it. This is similar to a person who copes with a great deal of pain in their body. Every day they wake up, and the moment they move, pain shoots through every part of their body. Minutes and sometimes hours pass before their body begins to turn off the pain receptors to their brains and normalize their body's functions, if at all.

Personally, I have dealt with pain in my body for more years now than I can remember. It is constant, and I refuse to take medications for fear of becoming dependent on them. I choose to depend on God for my healing. He has done it once before, and I know He will do it again. I am grateful to God that I do not struggle with the pain He has already healed in my body. My life would be so much more uncomfortable if He had not intervened on my behalf.

I will share that testimony with you, but before I do, I will tell you this process of enduring pain until the body hides it from you is the same process that our sin and shame use to hide from us. Eventually, we just forget that it ever happened and move on. But until we come to God with it and stand before His mirror, He cannot start that new work in us by planting the seeds of hope and forgiveness in our lives. Start now! Stand before God's mirror and ask Him to reveal to you what there is in your life that you may have forgotten about. Ask Him to show you every dark thing in your life, and then ask Him to replace it with His forgiveness, love, and light so that something new and full of life can grow where death and shame once lived.

My perspective of God's mirror comes from the pain I have endured for many years. A great portion of that pain was removed by God, and what remains will one day also be taken by God. The part that is gone was in my cervical spine. The story goes that when I was around nine years old, I was thrown out of the back of a moving pickup truck at around thirty miles an hour. Luckily for me, we were on the beach. It was the transition from the beach to the pavement that wound up ejecting me from the back of the truck. I landed headfirst in the sand. I do not remember any of the accident and only small pieces of the aftermath into the next day at the hospital when I woke up. What I do remember resulted in several injuries that had evolved into quite painful reminders.

In my early twenties, I began having quite a lot of pain in my cervical spine. This is generally the area of the neck between the base of the skull and the shoulders. I found that all of the discs between my vertebrae were herniated to some extent. During the therapy process, an X-ray revealed that I had, at some point in my life, broken my C1 vertebrae, which is the very first vertebrae near the base of the skull. After sharing the story of my accident, the therapist reviewing the X-ray proceeded to tell me that it stood to reason that I had a compression fracture there then. He also began to share with me that, had the dime-sized chip that broke off from the top of that vertebrae slipped back into the channel where my spinal cord resides, I could have been made a quadriplegic at the very best. He stated that death would have been most likely. However, instead of moving backward, it slipped forward and fused there, the entire injury resulting in the pain I was experiencing at that moment.

You might be thinking that this was a lucky break. I think it was so much more. I was picked up off of the beach by a bunch of guys who had no idea my neck was broken. I was laid in the floorboard of a van and driven the forty-five or so minutes back to civilization with half of my face missing, a tooth missing, and my lip ripped open to where you could see the entire top of my jaw line. I was then moved from that van to the back seat of my family's car, and then driven another thirty-five minutes to another town where the hospital was more capable of handling my injuries. The entire length of both trips, no one knew my neck was broken. I was then carried by my family into the emergency room and placed on a gurney. Again, no one knew my neck was broken.

The hospital I was taken to treated the wounds they could see. I do not remember having an X-ray done at that time, and neither does my mother. In any case, still no one knew I had a broken neck. I was moved repeatedly, asked to walk around, and had guests to my room, and for the next few weeks after the hospital, I went back to school and lived life like I fell off the bed. Still, no one knew I had a broken neck. I repeat the fact that no one knew I had a broken neck because it strikes me that bone can take several days to begin to heal, and the entire time I had a dime-sized slice of bone moving where it wanted to in my neck. God was there!

Moving forward to my twenties and the discovery of this, I was shocked. Instantly, I made all of these connections, and I began to refocus on God for the first time since I was a teen. I began to question God. I was asking questions like, "Why would you save my life only to make me live it in pain?" and "What do you want from me?" The reason I kept asking these questions had to do with some of the experiences I had with Christians up to this point in my life.

Please do not misunderstand me. I believe that most, if not all, Christians do what they do out of a sense that what they are doing is the right thing. What I have found, however, and what I hope this book helps to illuminate, is that what we "think" is right and what "is" right are two very distinct things. These two positions are often stark opposites. A person can do what they think is right and be so very wrong. Through the relationship with God that this book is endeavoring to share, we move from what we "think" to what God proves through His Word and through His love. If someone you are trying to share God with, or correct, cannot feel God's love through your words and actions, it is very possible that what you are doing is merely what you "think" is right. I encourage you to step back and ask God to reveal His path to you. Make sure that you can actually hear Him lead. Does the image in God's mirror look like you or Him?

My questions to God would, however, eventually be answered starting with my wife begging me to go to church with her. I was not having any of that, but she kept asking me. I had so many bad experiences with Christians that I simply did not want to be one. The last time I tried going to church, and when I met my wife, had resulted in yet another negative experience with the side of Christianity I wanted desperately to escape from. Therefore, I kept refusing her requests. She began going without me, and eventually I began to visit periodically with her. At this point, I was so far from God it felt like a million miles. There was no light from where I was standing. I was hurting physically, emotionally, and spiritually. There was, I thought, no reason for me to waste my time with Christianity. But judge not, lest ye be judged (**see Matthew 7:1**). And I was.

The Bible tells us that we can be sure that our sins will find us out. And boy, do they ever. During this decade or so of pain, introspection, and trial, my life felt as though it was upside down. The pain in my body was taking its toll, and the lack of sleep was making it worse. I was not a nice person to be around. I was one way at work and with friends, and a totally different person at home. What made things worse was that I was desperately trying to be better. I did not want to be those people from my past who had left a stain on God's love for me. I did not want to treat my wife, my kids, or anyone the way I had been treated as a kid. I especially did not want to treat my best friend and love of my life the way I had seen my mother treated. I tried repeatedly to treat my family the way my grandparents had treated me and each other. No matter what I did or how hard I tried, I failed. I truly did not know what love was.

In my early twenties, it was partly because of this that I eventually found myself dealing with an addiction to pornography. I had been unintentionally exposed to a collection of nude magazines at around five or six years old. This triggered a curiosity that turned into a need I did not want. I craved what appeared to be freely given and looked quite enjoyable. It wasn't until my late twenties or early thirties, while desperately trying to kick the habit, that I found a book by Andrew Fox titled *Real Sex Does Not Come from a Website: The Rewards of Pursuing Your Wife*. This book described how the images I had seen were, in most cases, forced. That most women did not want, or even desire, this kind of attention. The book even goes so far as to describe how women in the industry are either forced, drugged, or otherwise coerced into performing these lewd acts for the camera. Most become addicts because of it. In most cases, these women are unwilling participants in a sex trade that ultimately funds sex trafficking, drug trafficking, child slavery, and sex abuse, and ultimately, that money finds its way into funding terrorism.

I didn't want to believe it, so I went on to do an investigation of my own. The more I looked, the more I discovered that Mr. Fox was telling the truth. I found that a large number of the more famous female stars from the porn industry admitted later to being forced, drugged, and borderline raped to make the films they were in. Then I began to think about what that would mean if it was someone close to me. A sister, a daughter, or my own wife. I was disgusted. I begged God to change me. I begged Him for forgiveness. I decided then and there that I was not going to entertain this evil in my home or in my life. I educated my three sons on the same information. I told them what these images cost someone special, and I made it very clear that we were not going to support this kind of cruelty.

Looking back, I see that one of the reasons I took so heavily to porn was that I truly thought that that was what it looked like when a man and woman loved each other. I had no other evidence to the contrary. I had never seen a man truly court my mother with nothing expected in return. I had seen only men attempting to acquire my mother. Men in movies also seemed to only endeavor to acquire the beautiful love interest of the film. Divorce was always an option, and commitment was also optional. Films just seemed to reinforce the idea that if a relationship got tough, get another one. And, because as a teen I had given up on God, I had no example or desire to know what love really was.

However, I have always desired to court my wife, and I still do. There has never been a single doubt in my mind that she was the one for me. I can literally see my future in her eyes. It is as though I have met her somewhere before, and we have just not seen each other in a while. Each and every time I see her, I feel this way. We are, for all intents and purposes, best friends.

Early on in our relationship, and before Mr. Fox's book, I was doing things, and saying things, that did not honor her or God. I certainly was not bringing glory to God with my words and actions. And one day, it broke her. She had never been ok with pornography, but I had convinced her it was ok. Others had told us it was good for the relationship. That it added a little spice to the mix. They were all wrong. The only thing it did was drive a wedge between us. I would compare her and her actions in the bedroom to those in the videos. This was damaging to her, and it didn't make her want to be better or act differently: it made her not want to be around me. It damaged her self-esteem. She was now uncertain how to be what I thought I wanted. This image of intimacy was wrong. It was not life giving, and it only led to us being further apart emotionally.

My wife, who has always been so sweet, innocent, and close to God, knew it was wrong for pornography to be in our home. That single fact made it so much worse. She knew that we should never have entertained it. But our life had become all about me, what I wanted, what I was feeling, and what I wasn't getting. I had stopped courting my wife. I had stopped caring what she wanted, what she needed, and what she deserved. The mirror that pornography had placed in our relationship was showing us an image of intimacy that we should never have compared ourselves to. Those acts were not love. The things those people were doing were just self-fulfilling acts; they were chasing the desires of the flesh. Paul tells us in **Romans 1** that if we allow ourselves to be led by the lusts of the flesh and our selfish desires, God will turn us over to them, and we will be consumed. My wife knew it was wrong because she was closer to God's mirror. And honestly, I knew it too. But, because I had allowed myself to be led by my selfish

Chapter 5: Loving You

desires and lusts, God turned me over to them. The images were so enticing that I allowed myself to be pulled into that prison while the door slammed shut behind me, separating me from God, my wife, and my hope.

I had been a horrible person to her. And now, all of the judgment I had been passing down on those who I had deemed "failed examples of Christianity" from my past life in church was being poured back onto me. My wife was crushed. Her image of me had been shattered. Her trust in me was, I thought, gone. The one person in this world who was most precious to me, the one person who loved me because she wanted to, and not because there was a reason to, had been hurt because of my selfishness. And it hurt both of us.

But if you think that at this point I turned everything around, you would be so very wrong. I let this shame just turn into more hate, which caused more pain. One bad turn started another and that bus that had just run me over turned around and lined up for another pass. The really messed up thing about it was that I was driving the bus.

I began to attack the church. I demanded that she not go anymore. She refused, of course. I began to hate God. I already hated church, and now my marriage was on the rocks because yet again, God and His "church" were separating another marriage in my family, and I had had enough. I knew I wasn't going to get her to stop going, and I did not want to lose my wife to the church and its cult of self-righteous do-gooders, so I went. I did not participate. I sat staring at the preacher with the dirtiest look I could muster without drawing too much attention to myself. I would disrupt her experience so she would want to leave immediately after service. And I was all too eager to help her leave.

This went on for a couple of years until one Sunday my oldest son had an experience with God. Because of the way I had allowed the enemy to twist my thoughts, and even the way I perceived things, I did something that day that only God can forgive me for. I made my innocent son feel about two inches tall for talking to God that day. I tore into him and his mother with a fervor I never want to see again. I let them know in the meanest way possible that God was a liar and those people just wanted their money and had no intentions of helping you be better people. It was all a lie, and they were wasting their time trying. My son cried. I crushed him. I did that. I had officially become the thing I never wanted to be: killer of dreams for the ones I loved most in the world. And now, despite my efforts to the contrary, I was that thing. Now, tormented beyond belief, I was alone in the darkest of places. But this is still not where I turned around.

My wife was more desperate than I was to cling to her faith. Her grandmother was probably the most righteous person I have ever met. That spirit inside of me did not want to have anything to do with her, and so I tried not to. I did not like feeling that uncomfortable feeling whenever she was around. But, because of her, my wife kept going. She kept trying. She kept believing. She kept going to church, and I kept following.

In my late twenties and in terrible pain, barely able to turn my head, I sat in the pew angry. I was so angry at God that I did not want my wife to experience the Christianity that I had as a child. So I ran interference. I would go to church, sit in the pew, stare at the preacher, and, after making her just as uncomfortable as I was, we would leave. Then one Sunday night, I was doing that intimidation thing I was so dreadfully good at, and the preacher came up to me and asked me if he could pray for my neck. It was obvious by the way I walked and moved that I was hurting, and I am certain my wife had filled them in on just how bad. I told him he could do whatever he wanted to with as much disdain in my voice as I could muster. He prayed for me anyway, and of course, nothing happened. At this point, I was not surprised. I didn't expect anything to happen, I didn't deserve anything to happen, and I was so mad at God that I really didn't want Him to touch me. But He did!

I went home hurting the way I came to church. I spent the remainder of that evening uncomfortable as usual and trying to fall asleep in spite of the pain. About a month prior to this encounter, I had had an MRI done that showed all of the disks were ruptured and the spinal cord was pressed so hard against the spinal column that in the image, it was less than a sixteenth of an inch thick. The pain was excruciating. The doctors said that surgery was the only way to fix it. I told them they were never going to touch me. I had family members who had these back surgeries and were still in pain. Only now they could barely move. So no doctor was going to make my situation worse. And so every day I had to go to work, every day I had to live my life, and every night I would suffer through it. This night was no different. But God!

The next morning, I woke up as I usually did. I began my ritual of getting out of the bed, which required several deliberate movements to get my head up off of the pillow with the least amount of pain. It went something like this. I would grab the side of my head and hold it while turning my body onto one side. The idea being not to allow my head to turn contrary to my body. Then, once on my side, I would place a hand under my head while rolling out of the bed using my hand as a headrest to keep my head from staying on the pillow. That morning, I got to step two, and something was different. Normally, after step one, the searing pain would have me second-guessing my decision to wake up. I was most certainly, by that point, re-evaluating my decision to refrain from pharmacological assistance. However, that day, I felt no pain after step one. I proceeded with step two as a precaution, mainly out of disbelief, but also because I was uncertain as to what was happening. But once I had sat all the way up, I knew. I had been healed.

Why? I know, not really the question you might expect from someone who has had the miraculous happen to them, but that was mine. After all I had done. After the campaign of hate I had been taking out on God's church. After the things I had said to my wife and son. After how I had made them feel about their belief in Him. Why me? Why now? And then, I broke.

Before the end of that day, one that I will never forget, I turned and faced God and His mirror for the first time since I was a teen. I didn't turn to Him to see if He was there—no, this time I knew He was. This time I turned to Him in total submission. I turned to Him with complete belief in who He was. I looked to Him to tell me what to do, where to go, and how to go about doing it. I was totally invested in what God had to say to me. Why this time? Because I had nothing to lose and everything to gain. I did not deserve what He had done for me. Yet He did it anyway. I had not earned the forgiveness required for Him to even look at me, but by His grace He did. He came to me where I was. He came to me in my affliction. He changed my life for the better despite my total dedication to making His life worse. He showed me something that day when I looked in His mirror. He showed me true love for the first time ever. A father, who gave a gift of love, even though nothing had been done or given to deserve it. He showed me a glimpse of who He had called me to be. A loving father, husband, and friend.

Next

Standing in front of God's mirror will show us a lot of things, but the most important thing it shows us is His forgiveness. Without this, we cannot achieve our next. We cannot walk confidently away from who we once were to the new person He is calling us to be. But if we are willing to listen to what He has to say and commit to the sacrifices required, we will fulfill His calling on our lives.

Some of us may be called to lead a church, but all of us are called to ministry. As a believer who is standing before God's mirror, you are called to share that image with those around you. Believe it or not, that is a ministry, and you are a natural at it. Just be the new you that God has created, and His light and His Spirit will take care of the rest. Part of loving yourself is knowing and accepting that what God has done is to change who you were into who He created you to be. There is no one better suited to be the light to your friends and family than you. Who can love people who already love you more than you can? Accept your calling. Stand before God's mirror and walk into your next as He guides you. Let His Spirit that He has placed inside of you open your heart to the new thing He is doing in your life and in the lives of those around you. It is not too far-fetched to believe that the God who heals can also make something new. Is it?

Standing in front of His mirror looking out over my next, I see a new man. I see a man who has not dishonored his wife and best friend. I see a man who loves her with everything that he is. A man who would lay down his life for her without question. I see a man who loves his kids the same way. The man I see loves God with everything he is, in spite of everything he is not. I feel a love that I cannot explain. I hear a voice that I never want to walk away from. I feel security in His presence, hope for the future, and peace and joy in the present. It is as if the past never happened. Old things are washed away, and everything has been made new.

Those whom I have done wrong surely have not forgotten what I have done. I have not forgotten what I have done. But oddly, the shame of what I have done is gone. I feel no condemnation for my past, only love and forgiveness. I live each new day with the possibility of proving God in my life to those I have wronged. I wake up in the morning, and I am better than the day before. My life with my wife evolves each day. The desire inside of me to be the best father I can be for my children is renewed every day. I wake up with the determination to do better than the day before. I love to show my kids the love of God, and because of that, they truly get to experience the change God has made in me.

Whatever you think you have done that is so bad that you think forgiveness is a pipe dream, let it go. Start dreaming. I placed God in a box for too long. Don't make that same mistake. A love like God's transcends fault. It covers sin. God can be the God of the Old Testament. He can be the brutal, fire and brimstone God we read about. But I do not believe that He desires to be that God for those who believe. Many times in the Scripture, we see where God desires a relationship with us. And every time, we see that He can only find one or two who are willing to do what it takes to bridge the gap between sin and righteousness to be in God's presence. From my experience, God reached out to me. God took the first steps to be my friend. To love me while I was still a sinner. If God will reach down into my filthy, self-destructive, and selfish life so full of sin, do you not believe that He would do the same for you? I do.

Next is simply about where you want to go from here. Since here is now a new place, the possibilities are endless. The consequences of your choices may still be yours to pay, but the parts of your old life that were keeping you from God are gone. The parts of your life that were keeping you from experiencing and giving true love are also gone. Even if the things you have done in your past have caused you to be physically imprisoned, God will not leave you there to rot and stew in your misery. He works all things out for the good of those who love Him and are called according to His goodness and mercy (**see Romans 8:28**). If you truly love Him, then you are standing in front of that mirror. If you are standing in front of that mirror, you are intentionally asking God what there is about you that needs to change before He can use you.

Once you get there, I believe He will use you in a mighty way. And if God is using you, then you are called. That means that even your time in prison can be used for your benefit and the benefit of others who also believe in Him. So if this is you, fulfill the calling that God has placed on your life, and minister God's love and mercy to those who need it most. You were placed there for such a time as this. Be the person God has called you to be. Lay down your life for a friend. Spend the time God has given you making sure that someone else knows Him like you do. Without judgment, without condemnation, and without sin. Let that someone know that all they are required to do to know God is believe. He will take care of the rest if they are willing to follow Him. But one question remains: are you willing to follow Him?

I am the only one I have control over. I cannot change you, and you cannot change me. God can do whatever He wants to. But because He loves us, He allows us to choose our own path. If we choose Him, He is faithful to bless and honor our choice. But if we choose to tread elsewhere, He will not just strike us down. He will not simply punish us because we did not listen to Him. He is patient and kind. He will wait and watch as we endure pain and suffering all the while hoping that we will reach out for Him. If we do, He will come to our aid and protect us from evil. God Himself will never tempt you with evil. He will never try to seduce you with the things He has told you are a sin. But He will also not stand in the way of your choices. He wants you to choose, and He so desperately wants you to choose Him.

Now that I am a new man, I am focused on changing myself. I stand in front of God's mirror daily, and I ask the same questions every day. What do I still have in my life that does not honor you? What do I need to change? And will you give me strength, O God, that I might succeed for your glory? I do not fear the past. I do not hide in the present. If I make a mistake, I own it. I will tell the truth, even if it hurts me. But God is faithful. And I truly believe that because it is the desire of my heart to honor Him, He blesses me when I do. He has proven this to me time and again.

Throughout my late twenties, thirties, and early forties, I ran an IT consulting business for more than fifteen years. While doing so, I made several mistakes. Why wouldn't I? I am human, after all. In each instance, I chose to tell the truth rather than lie to cover my mistake. Each time, I accepted the consequences and moved on. I never lost a client because of a mistake. My business grew each year until I had more than 450 clients. God was faithful to bless me when I honored Him and without fail. How do I know? I never advertised my business. It was all word of mouth. God is good! In fact, when I first began really studying God's Word and moving in closer to Him, there was an employee at one of my clients' shops who suddenly began calling me "preacher" when I would walk past him in the shop. We did not know each other outside of that environment, but he saw something in me that, at the time, I did not.

It is moments like those that confirm God's presence in my life. Those moments confirm the new man that God has created. God's mirror helps me to be reminded daily that I am who He made me to be. That daily stop reminds me that the creator of all things, our God, loves me. He loves me! That daily routine gives me joy each morning. It renews my hope that by the end of the day, God will have spoken to me and used me in some way. I look forward to those moments with God. I long to hear His voice. I desire to do whatever He asks me to do, whatever that may be. I no longer hold back from God. I no longer stand with fear, while trying to move forward in Him. I am free! He has set me free! And there is nothing in existence that will be allowed to put those chains back on me ever again.

Freedom

Freedom. No matter where you live, freedom holds meaning. It is oftentimes sought after, relished, and revered. One word that means the difference between bondage and ability. Freedom of religion, freedom of speech, freedom from oppression, freedom from fear, freedom from ... Whatever you want freedom from, it can be yours, but sacrifice will be required. No, not like killing-and-bleeding-an-animal type sacrifice. Sacrifice of effort, time, money, family, and sometimes even our very lives. But with God, freedom is free.

It is another one of those overcomplicated situations. Interesting how we humans seem to take the simplest ideas and ideals and complicate them to the point where they require more than we are willing to give. More than we can even offer. God, however, does not complicate anything. He simplifies everything by telling us exactly what is required. He even helps us obtain what is necessary for Him to move. If we need righteousness, He gives us faith. If we want freedom, He gives us forgiveness. We quite literally sit in a cell of our own making with the door unlocked and wide open, screaming to God to let us out of the cage we are in. Seriously! I have made this mistake in the past. I have lost so many years to fear and uncertainty, thinking that the cage I was in was punishment from God, or God ignoring my pleas, when the door was open the entire time.

The type of freedom offered by God covers the entire gamut of freedom available. If you need freedom from an oppressor, pray God's forgiveness for that person. What better way for someone who is in fact in their own prison of fear and self-doubt to be absolved of the shame caused by their own choices and actions than forgiveness. Simple, right?

If you are needing freedom from addiction, ask for forgiveness, wisdom, and strength. God will take away the shame of your past actions and choices with forgiveness and love. He will give freely His divine wisdom so that your future choices can be filtered through Him. Pray for strength so that while you are in dark moments of temptation, God will be faithful to send His angels to your side and hold up your arms in the midst of your battles. If you do not know, that is a reference to the Old Testament in **Exodus 17** when Moses was required to keep his hands raised to God so that Israel would continue to win the battle they were fighting. When he grew weary, his arms were heavy and he was unable to keep them in the air. But he had help who came to his side and held his arms up for him so that the battle would be won. God will be faithful to do this for you. All you have to do is ask, believing that it will be done.

My friend Pastor Andrew was having some pretty major health issues one year, and our men's group went to a conference for the weekend. While at that conference, we had a prayer session in a particular place on the campground where God had repeatedly answered prayers. People had been healed there in that spot, and so while at prayer, we all began praying for our pastor. With him in our midst, we began praying, and I remembered that story of Moses. I began to tell God I was not going to quit praying until my pastor was healed. I was not going to put down my arms until He answered my prayer. I don't know how long we were out there, but it was several hours. I remember some of the guys mentioning the length of that prayer session because it was one of the longest they had ever hosted out there. But while we were praying, I refused to put my arms down. I kept them up the entire time. I prayed, I cried, we cried. My arms began to burn so bad as if they were on fire. The joints hurt, and my neck began to hurt as my muscles began to spasm from the strain. I refused to give up. My arms remained up, and while we were praying, others from the group saw that I had my arms up in the air, and they came over to pray with me. Believing that I was in prayer with God for something, and not knowing what, they began to pray with me. As they did, they unconsciously began to hold up my arms. God saw the desire of my heart and sent my brothers to help me win the battle. And we did. Pastor Andrew left that prayer circle feeling better than he ever had and began to return to normal from then on. Did it have anything to do with my prayer? I would like to believe so, but even if not, I saw God move that day, and that was miracle enough for me.

Our new man through Christ loves to see God move. He longs for it. When God moves, we are overwhelmed with joy and a peace that Scripture says passes all understanding (**see Philippians 4:7**). It's peace that we cannot even imagine. Is it any wonder that our new man desires this experience? I find myself every day looking for God. Looking for His fingerprints in my life. Searching for His miracles. Why? Because I relish the opportunity to see it and share it with someone else.

At the beginning of my walk as a new man, I did not want to pray for people. I was embarrassed by my lack of eloquent prayer. I was allowing the enemy to influence my new man. The enemy was attempting to entrap and once again cage my new man, but I was unwilling to allow him to do so. I stood my ground, and I began to ask God what He wanted me to do. God directed me to Jesus's example of prayer (**see Matthew 6:1-15**).

Shortly after the men's event at the campgrounds, I was invited, for the first of three times, to participate in an organization called Christian Warriors Retreat. It is an organization that caters to veterans and first responders. It started as a men's retreat, and now there is a women's retreat and a wives retreat. The purpose of this group is to show God's love to a hurting and wounded warrior who, without God, has been trapped by the enemy into believing that there either is no God or that their actions or past have put them in a place where God cannot reach them. Oh, what a lie!

When I was invited to serve with this group, the enemy immediately began attacking me. He was intent on convincing me that I was not good enough to be a part of an organization for veterans because I had never sworn in. One of only two male members of my family to not join up, I was already dealing with that decision and what it must have looked like to my grandfathers and my dad, whom I loved very much. I honor them every day with my words and my actions. I show the world that, despite my treacherous childhood, I was not a victim. I am not a product of fear and hate, I am a child of the most high God, and because of their honorable presence in my life when I needed it most, I am. But I let the enemy get to me.

As brand-new believers in God, we have not yet matured into the calling of God. We are still learning to listen for and hear the voice of God. The enemy knows this and will do what he can to get in our way. I was asked to join and even speak at the Christian Warriors Retreat two years later, and I still let the enemy get in my head.

Despite the enemy's constant attacks, when asked a third time, I decided to join this group, and do you know what they asked me to do first? Be on the prayer team. Shortly before I had been told what I would be doing on retreat, I was also approached by one of the pastors in our church and asked to be on the prayer team there. I told her I would have to "pray" about it. You know, the answer you give when you don't want to offend, but you're probably going to say no anyway. Well, now with two different people asking me to be on a prayer team, I ran at it with everything I had.

While on retreat that first time, and every time since, I have seen God move in the lives of the men I respect and honor because of their sacrifice to defend one of the most valuable things on this planet: freedom. I have been present not for the torment of the enemy that held them down, but for the all-important moment when their lives were forever changed. I have seen chains fall from their arms. I have watched as God removed the shame and guilt for things of their past and things they had to do in the operation of their duties as warriors for freedom. God has never failed them, and He has never failed me. Each time I pray, He has always allowed me to see what my prayer does. It means so much to me to be able to pray for people now, to watch as they achieve freedom, or healing, or find God for the first time. God is good! And He always knows what's best for us. Even when we can't see it ourselves. We just need to stay in front of His mirror and keep praying. Keep communicating with Him.

In our efforts to learn to love ourselves, it is important to remember that loving God is key. If we stop honoring God with all we are, we begin to slip out from in front of His mirror. When we do, our filter gets broken. Without it, our decisions become more self-serving, our words lose wisdom and love, and our actions become meaningless. Without God's filter, we lose purpose. Without purpose, we begin to feel disconnected. I never again want to step away from God's mirror.

God, help us to always seek you. Help us to know you intimately that we might see, through you, our purpose. Help us to know who we are in you so that your Spirit can work through us and by working with us, and through us, we might know your love for us. Make your love for us the example by which we, free from shame and guilt, learn to love ourselves. Through Christ Jesus I pray, Amen.

Chapter 6
LOVING THEM

Loving others is not an easy thing to do. It requires so much more patience and grace then I can sometimes muster. God knew this, which is why I believe He made sure that we needed to love Him and ourselves first. Standing before God's mirror and learning, through intimate relationship with Him, that we truly are His children and that He loves us unconditionally, allowing Him the opportunity to prove it and spending time with Him in perfect unity of Spirit: without these intimate moments with Him, we would never know who we are. We would never have learned what our purpose was. How could we?

Trying to love someone who, perhaps, has not gone through the process of learning who they are through a relationship with God can be challenging. They usually have no direction, no idea who they are or what their purpose is, and they will most likely have a deep-seated distrust of themselves and others. This results in a lot of shame, hate, and fear to overcome. The first thing we have to know when approaching others is that it is not our job to change them.

I know, as Christians, the first thing we seem to be taught is that we need to go out into our circle of influence and "save" them. Some will hear that and they want to go to their friends and family and inform them of everything that they are doing that is not Christ-like and how if they don't change their ways, they are most likely going to hell because of it. Others will hear the same call to action and want to go to those people and quote Scripture and try to drag them to church every chance they get. I know this because I have been both.

What I have learned through my relationship with God is that these people already know what they have been doing wrong. We all do. Seriously! Stop right now and think about all the things you do on a daily basis. Which ones are wrong? See what I mean? My friends and family do not need another judge; they need a Christ-like friend. They need someone who can help them over the difficult parts of their own walk with God. The Bible says that everything in all of creation cries out to Him (**see Revelation 5:13**). In fact, it says that if we don't, the rocks will (**see Luke 19:40**). Wow!

Knowledge of God is not the only thing required to be a Christ-like example to our circles of influence. We also need to have an intimate relationship with Him. We need to not just know of Him but have a personal relationship with Him. We need to know His voice without doubt. We need to also know who we are in Him, through Him, and to Him. When we can truly answer those questions, I believe that we are then able to tap into a whole new realm of God's divine nature and power. So much so that when we are simply in the presence of our friends and family, they are in the presence of God's Holy Spirit, and they know it. By simply being present, we become God's examples to those we choose to spend time with. This is exactly what we are supposed to be to them: His light.

When I stopped trying to change the people around me, but instead loved them with the same unconditional love with which God loves me, something began to happen. The people around me began to make different choices without me telling them anything. They began to think of themselves differently. They began to be healed of their sicknesses and began finding new hope in the midst of their struggles.

Change

None of these things were because of me, but rather in spite of me. God did these things for those who were seeking Him, just like Scripture says He will (**see Hebrews 11:6**). The reason we get to see it happening is because we have chosen to die to ourselves daily and we allow God to "love" through us.

Our immediate natural reaction to someone who is being offensive or someone who is acting, speaking, or living in a way contrary to our own beliefs is to judge them for it. We immediately want to share with them all of the things that they were doing wrong and why. We want to make sure that their behavior is corrected so that we don't have to endure any more of it. Where is God in that?

We are told to die to self daily, not just because we need to avoid the sin of our own words and actions, but also because we need to avoid the sin of being judgmental, of entertaining a spirit of offense, and of thoughts that are not honoring or virtuous to God. We have become so incredibly used to having the ability to look at someone, listen to their rhetoric, and make an assumption as to their character without ever having a relationship with that person. Without the benefit of relationship, we lose the most important perspective of who someone really is: their heart.

Some of the people in my life who made me the most uncomfortable in their presence and whom I tried to avoid entirely have done some of the greatest work in God's kingdom. They have reached more people and changed more lives than I ever have. I tried to live the Christian life of my youth avoiding people who I saw as living an unholy or unrighteous life. I did these things because I had been taught to do so by the doctrines of some of the denominations I have been a part of. Their belief was that if they avoided allowing sinners into their inner circles, they would avoid the temptation to sin themselves. At the risk of sounding judgmental, while they were partially correct, they were also majorly wrong.

How were they right? The Scripture says that we can judge the actions of other believers, but it must start with us (**see 1 Peter 4:17**). If there are any among us in the body of Christ who are not living according to the gospel, we are to correct them in love. For example, if you know someone in your congregation who is a member of the church and who has made the declaration of belief in Christ, but because of a personal relationship with them, you know of sin they may be committing, then you are told to pray for them and correct them with God's love and help them find their way back to the path of righteousness through forgiveness (**see James 5:16, 19-20**). It never says that you are supposed to go tell another member of the congregation what that person is doing. That instruction is only for when a brother or sister has sinned against you, and in order to keep unity, you share what is going on with a leader and then the pastor, but only after trying to talk to the person directly first (**see Matthew 18:15-17**).

This brings us to the primary ways in which those doctrines were wrong. How can either of the two things above happen if you do not first invest time and effort into a relationship with the other members of your church body? If you do not have a relationship with the person sinning, I have two questions for you. First, how do you know they are sinning? Was it because they sinned against or with you? Second, do you have a close personal relationship with the person sinning? If by answering the first question, you find that your knowledge of their activities is either gossip or judgment, then let you who is without sin cast the first stone. If you find by answering the second question that you have no relationship with them that contains love, then anything you say to them will cause offense and therefore cause you both to have sinned. Relationship first and then correction. The wounds of a friend can be trusted (**see Proverbs 27:6**). Everything else just causes pain.

These are the things that God has been illuminating to me that I was doing wrong. I cannot change you. Just like you cannot change me. Separately, we can change ourselves, and then together we can change the world. Jesus and His disciples were an example of this.

Jesus worked on Himself, His example showed these other twelve men how they should live, and they each worked on themselves. When they tried to change others, Jesus would often correct them and share with them the perils of judgment. Judge not lest you also be judged (**see Matthew 7:1**). Ringing any bells?

When a person who needs Jesus speaks or acts, the things they say and do are going to cause the spirit that God created inside our new selves to rise up with a righteous indignation. I believe this happens, in part, so that we know that these things are wrong. Another reason this happens is because if the light of God is truly inside of us, then when in the presence of darkness, a spiritual battle ensues. When this battle begins, we can sense the presence of darkness and the evil it tries to hide. But because darkness flees in the presence of the light, evil's hiding place has been destroyed, and it is not happy. With sin now illuminated, we are brought to a choice. Judge the sin and love the sinner, or just judge the sinner because of the sin. If God is in you, ask God to show you the heart of the sinner. If you do, you may be surprised to find that there is a scared little boy or girl in there hiding in the corner of their flesh, terrified of the darkness that has taken over. And the only thing needed to set them free of that darkness is the love of God that you have been so graciously given. Why not save that soul by giving away freely what was given to you freely: the love, grace, mercy, and forgiveness of God through Christ Jesus?

Hope

Change brings hope. When a person who has been lost is found, they are usually overwhelmed with the joy of not being lost anymore. The hope of a future is restored in their lives, and they long to make new connections and restore old ones. When a person who has done someone wrong is forgiven, a weight rises from their shoulders as if someone has taken something heavy off of them. With that change, hope of what's yet to come and of new life begins to grow inside of them.

I remember when I had hurt my wife emotionally and spiritually early in our marriage. It placed upon me a crushing weight of guilt and pain. My life was changed. It seemed only fair since I had caused her life to be changed as well. I felt so guilty for what I had said and done that I carried that guilt around with me as a reminder of what a trash person I was for doing so. That decision led to more pain, more fear, more anger, and more division in my home and then began to spill over into other relationships. All because I was too angry at myself to think I could ever have been forgiven. How could I be? Why would she ever forgive me? How could I forgive me?

I held onto that anger and pain for almost a decade. It was mine. I had done it, and I was going to accept responsibility for what I had done. I was going to stand up and take the punishment I deserved. Why shouldn't I? I had been raised to believe that what I sowed I would reap. I sowed pain and suffering, and so I was reaping pain and suffering. I was not happy with what I was going through, what we were going through, but I created this prison. I had to live in it. Right?

Wrong! While yes, I will reap what I sow, and we all will, I do not have to suffer with it. If I truly seek forgiveness for a wrong I have committed, the Bible says I will receive it. It does not say that I can avoid the consequences of my actions, merely that I will be forgiven for what I have done. In other words, the sin of what I have done will be forgiven and then forgotten by God. If the change in my life is consistent and evident to those around me, then the forgiveness of that sin that I seek from them will also be granted. The Scripture says that God will make even my enemies to be at peace with me (**see Proverbs 16:7**). So forgiveness of sin will be freely given.

But I am my own worst enemy. I hold the longest, most intense grudges against me than anyone else on this earth ever could. And I did not want to forgive me. I did not deserve forgiveness. And because I felt that way, I could not ask for forgiveness. But God!

God kept calling to me, and through His efforts, I slowly drew closer. As I got closer to His light, my sins were beginning to be uncovered from their dark hiding places. Knowing that I could never get closer to God carrying all of these sins around, I knew I had to make a choice: follow Him or stay in the dark where I was. It was a moment that felt like when I was a child and I called out to my mother in the dark. Though my bedroom door was closed, when she turned on the light in the hall or bathroom, the light came flooding into my room through the crack in the door. This is how God's love for us is. When we call out to Him, the light comes on, and no matter how small the crack in our prison door is, the light always shines through. God is faithful to forgive, and He did.

When I called out to God, He did not wait to come to my call. He opened up His heart and the love that poured out on me was intense. His light illuminated the parts of me that I did not like, and I began to change them one at a time. As I did, I found that the path to forgiveness was being blocked by me. This created a difficult situation where I had to come to terms with what I had done and let it go. God gave me the choice. I chose God.

God came into my life like a flood, washing away everything that was not of Him. My words began to change. My actions began to change. It was as if I was literally a new man. The only thing required of me for this to happen was that I believe in Him. This always takes me back to the moment in church as a child when I had my first encounter with God. I was told at the time that I needed to try harder, that I was almost there, but not quite. Each time, I tried to pray harder, I tried to cry more, I tried to be what I thought God wanted me to be because that was what I had been told I needed to do. Those people meant well, and they were only trying to help, but when I met God this time, on His terms, the only thing I did was believe He was there and that He had my best interest at heart. I truly believed, like I had when I was a child. I believed that God was the creator of everything, that He did send Jesus to become a sacrifice for my sin, and that if I believed, I would have everlasting life through Him. He met me there.

Over time, God has shown me that all that is required of us to love others is that we need to love Him first. Then we learn to love ourselves the way He loves us, and at that point we will love others in the best possible way. By simply obeying the greatest commandment to love God with all we are, we then have learned how to obey the second, which is to love our neighbor as ourselves (**see Matthew 22:36-40**). The only thing I need to be for someone hurting and in pain is love. Love is hope. God's perfect love has the power to cast out all fear (**see 1 John 4:18**).

New Life

Hope brings new life, a restoration. When we as Christians are intentional about our walk with God, He will be faithful to bring us to the people and places where we are needed to bring and be hope to those who have forgotten how to believe. Whether it is life that broke them or someone or something else, God responds when they call out to Him. It is not a reserved hope. It is not an "only if" kind of hope. God is love, and His love is hope. Hope grows in God's love. Wherever God is, there is hope. Wherever God is, there is freedom. Through His hope and freedom, chains are loosed, prison doors swing open, and lives are forever changed. Healing our mind, body, and spirit begins with God's eternal hope.

When Christians, living as God has called us to live, bring our belief in Him to those who have lost theirs, we do not need to point out their faults and how much more righteous we are than them. They do not need to be told how wrong they are; they already know. Because they know how wrong they are, they have lost hope. They have forgotten the way back to God. They are in that dark place and crying out in their spirits to God. We need to have a relationship with them so that when they call out to God, we can be His light shining through the crack in their prison door. When they call out, we can respond in love instead of judgment. Why is it so hard for us to keep our thoughts and our tongue under control? Why is it that our flesh regularly gets the better of us and we begin to sink like Peter did?

Like Peter, we see the wind and waves. We see the sin that is right in front of us, and we forget that we are to love the sinner to God. We are to show them how to live for God through our words and our actions. But we keep allowing their sin to distract us from God's plan. God's goodness and mercy was good enough for us. His grace was good enough for us. Why do we so easily think that this sinner before us is just too far gone? Were we?

God came to us all in the midst of our trouble; in the midst of our sin, we heard Him call to us. Jesus died to cover the sins that we were not yet even born to make. He knew us before our mothers did, and yet somehow we think that we know more than God, that somehow our judgment is going to stick when God made a way for even His judgment to fall away from us.

Loving your neighbor as yourself is a testament to how much God loved us. God loved the whole world, even those who were not yet born, so much that He gave His only Son. He did that for you. He did that for me. He did that for those you haven't even met yet. And He did it so that if we would just believe in Him, we could have everlasting life. What kind of person gives so much for so very little? Can you? In **John 15**, Jesus said that no greater love has any man than that he lay down his life for his friends. This is exactly what Jesus did. Knowing what was about to happen to Him, He did it anyway.

All God is asking us to do is stand before our friends and family and believe. He is not asking you to move mountains. He said you could if you wanted to, but He never said you had to. He never said you have to heal people, but you can if you believe. All God wants us to do is believe. If you can believe, you can love. If you can love, you can bring God's light to the darkness. And if you can bring God's light to those in dark places, you bring hope to the world. All you have to do to accomplish this life-giving and world-changing feat: believe.

The only questions we should have in our minds and in our hearts are: Who am I that God loved me? And who am I that I might love others? A sinner lost without God just needs to know that there is someone out there who genuinely cares whether they live or die. They need to know that there is someone out there who wants to spend time getting to know them. And they need to know more than anything that once they let you in, you're still going to love them. Regardless of the filth in their life. Regardless of the sin they have committed. You are going to stand by them through the consequences. They need to know that you and I are going to love them the way God does.

God's love brings new life. God's love brings hope, joy, and peace. Does yours? If we are truly Christ-like, then I believe it should. I am not perfect. I struggle to die to myself every day. I wake up the same way you probably do, still tired, aching, and well aware of the struggles the day is about to throw at me. I see, before I open my eyes, the pain in my body, the family struggles and drama that are destined for the day, and even the financial and business-related tasks that will most likely overwhelm me that day. Dying to myself means I have to lay all of that at the feet of Jesus and believe that He will intercede for me. I need to believe that come what may, I am loved so much that I will not suffer but thrive in spite of what may come. Tomorrow was not promised, but today, God's got this.

Once I have my selfish thoughts and worries under control and given to God, I can then focus on the needs and desires of those around me. What does my wife need today? What can I do to serve her and the kids today? What does my church need? What do my friends and neighbors need? What does my community need? How can I show God's love to all of these? How can I lay down my life for all of these the way Jesus did for me? Am I living out the calling of God in my life?

These questions are not difficult to answer once we realize that we do indeed believe in God, that God is love, and He loves us. We can then forgive and love ourselves, and God has called us to love and forgive those He brings into our lives. The hardest part is getting to the place where you wake up and first ask these questions. I still struggle with this, but God is faithful to complete the work He started in me. God is my ever-present help in my time of need. He will never leave me or forsake me. There is no need for me to fight the battle of my life that He is more than capable of fighting for me. If I believe, follow His lead, and trust Him, my day will go exactly the way He planned it to, leaving me free to do what He asked me to, which is to love my neighbor as myself.

When was the last time you trusted Him? When was the last time you truly and unconditionally loved? Have you forgiven those who have done you wrong? Have you forgiven yourself? Do you truly and unconditionally love yourself as Christ did? Do you love others the same way?

Unconditional Love

If we who are called will love the way we are instructed to in our Bibles, then the new life that is born from loving others will also create life. Everlasting life will spring up from the lives of those we have influenced. Their words will begin to bring life into the lives of those in their circles. Their actions will begin to honor God, and we will have fulfilled our purpose by helping those around us to find and fulfill theirs. We will create disciples who will make disciples.

Unconditional love is the love God gave to us in the beginning, before we first believed in Him. He gave us that unconditional love before we were even born. Before our parents, or their parents, even as far back as you can think: He has always loved us unconditionally. He has given us so much and required so very little in return. We get caught up in our own problems, our own lack, and we forget that all we have to do is believe. Then, if we believe, He will give us whatever we ask for. The problem was never that we had problems, or lacked certain necessities, or even whether God was there or not. The problem was that we simply did not believe.

Now that we believe; have been given faith; have learned to love God with all our heart, mind, and soul; and have learned to forgive and love ourselves the way He loves us, we can use that gift to love others. We can use what God has taught us, and continues to teach us, to show others how to believe. We can show them who God is, what He is capable of, and just how very much He loves them. If we can do that, then they can start down the path we are already on and learn the same things we have learned. They will even have the same close relationship with God that we have.

The way I try to love on others is to show them who God is to me. I pray for the sick, and they get well. I pray for hope for those without it, and they are restored. My own son lay in a hospital bed once, hooked up to all sorts of machines. I prayed and asked others to pray with me; while we prayed, I watched the machines, whose numbers had been dropping rapidly—indicating I was about to lose my son—suddenly stop dropping and begin to improve. He made a full recovery. I made sure to let him know that God had a hand in his healing, to give God the glory. My son sleeps with the blinds open in his room now, for no other reason except that he wants to be reminded of God as the sun rises and shines through his window every morning. His words, not mine.

Without God's love, we are empty shells. Without love, we have no purpose. We have no meaning. No reason to exist. Love is the life force that runs through our veins. It was a free gift from God, and if we apply it correctly to our lives, it will be a free gift to those around us. We can change the world one heart at a time. We can show our brothers and sisters how much they mean to God by letting them know every day, despite their failings, what their value is.

Praise the giftings of others. Not in a way that is flattering, but in a way that is meaningful. For example, if you see that someone you know has a gift with organization, praise them for it, and invite them to organize something for you. In other words, don't just say you like what they can do; show them. Make it valuable to you. Maybe even pay them for what they can do and encourage them to make money on the side doing it for others. If they decide to do that, put the word out and help them get started by marketing their efforts on social media and in person. If it truly has value, then you should have no problem making sure other people know.

On the other hand, don't tell someone they are good at something if they are not. You are setting them up for failure. Where is the love in that? If they are truly passionate about something, but seem to have no talent with it, don't just tell them they are terrible at it; help them try. Maybe you know someone who is good at it. Help get them the practice, the training, or the opportunity they need to at least try. If they still fail, then at least they have a great friend who stood by them for the entire experience and now have someone to talk to about how and why and next steps. The worst thing you can do to someone who is trying something new is to walk away in the middle of the effort. When you do, you leave them with the worry and the stress of not knowing. The added weight can cause them to sink and maybe even fail. Guess who they will remember left them hanging? Yep ... you.

A true friend sticks closer than a brother (**see Proverbs 18:24**). If you are truly someone's friend, you are going to love them through everything. The bad times might just mean addiction, destructive behavior, or even hateful words and actions directed at you. If you are really their friend, you will give them time to cool off and welcome them back. Even if the apology comes from you. Loving someone unconditionally means taking blame when there is none to be had on your part. Loving someone means allowing them to go when you prefer they stay.

Jesus's disciples and friends were not perfect. They made mistakes. After all, they were tax collectors, prostitutes, and sinners. I can only imagine how much love Jesus had to have for Judas knowing what he was going to do to Him later. Yet the entire time he walked with Jesus, not a word was said about his failures. Jesus loved him. I imagine Jesus loved him to the point where He hoped Judas would change his mind. It is said that Judas would steal from the disciples' coffers. He had an enormous problem with greed. Whatever the root of his problem was, Jesus still showed Judas love.

Peter denied Jesus, yet Jesus gave him an opportunity for redemption and then built the entire Christian church on Peter and the relationship between the two of them. Sin, redemption, and forgiveness are perpetually embodied in the story of how Peter fell short, was redeemed, was then forgiven, and was ultimately given authority over other believers. When you read the rest of the story, you see how Peter was still not perfect and he continued to fall short, but he never stopped trying. And when it came time for Peter to be crucified like Jesus, he requested they hang him upside down. Why? Because he said he was not worthy of even the same torture as Jesus. Peter knew he was not perfect. He knew that he consistently failed God. His efforts did not stop just because he fell short of the mark. He got up again, and again, and kept trying to fulfill the calling Jesus had given him.

Like Peter, our friends and family know when, how often, and how many times they have failed us. They know they are not perfect. They also know that we are not perfect. They do not need those who are claiming to love them constantly judging them and reminding them of everything they've done wrong or every time they've failed. They need people in their lives just like Jesus who, despite their failures, are going to love and empower them, people who will not give up on loving them, or trusting them, simply because they failed. The focus should be on whether or not they are trying. Are they trying to do better and just can't quite make it over the hill to their next? Are they trying to change the way they live, act, talk, or play and just can't break free from the old crowd or bad habits? If so, I have one question for you. How can you help?

The Bible says no greater love has anyone than to lay down his life for a friend (**see John 15:13**). What better reason to lay down your life, your desires, your wants, and your perceived future than to lay it all down to help a friend get over that hill, to climb that mountain they keep staring at? What better way to show them that you indeed care and that love is all you have for them? Show them that because you believe so completely in what God has promised you, you're willing to share the one thing you have so little of: your time. Whatever they need of it is theirs. When they are sick, pray for them to be healed. When they are not around, pray God's blessing and favor on them and God's peace for the mind, body, spirit, and day. Let them know publicly just how much they mean to you. Take up the hard conversations and breathe God's love, wisdom, and life into them. If not you, then who?

Love like there is no tomorrow, and pray like you need one more.

Chapter 7
CONCLUSION

Unity of Belief

You might ask, "How? How do we give so much when we ourselves struggle?" By living our lives as holy examples. By being the light of God in a dark world. If people are speaking hate, we speak love. If death is on the horizon, we speak life. If darkness tries to take over our families, our homes, or our nations, we show them God's light.

I heard it said once that when we go out into the world to spread the good news of Jesus, we should use our actions. We need to let those who need Him see Him through our works. And, if necessary, use words. It is claimed that St. Francis of Assisi said this, but there is some controversy as to whether this is true. What he did write was, "... let all [terms vary] preach by their deeds." When I heard it quoted, though, I thought, "Brilliant!" That is exactly who I feel called to be: a person of action. Not of violence, or force, but of goodness and peace. Not a pushover, but one who knows what they believe and believes it with conviction. I see too many people of other religions and of other beliefs who live their lives with such conviction about what they believe. I see them and I think, "Why not me?"

It is so very important that we stand for something we believe in. I believe that God is real. I know that He heals. I know that He moves in special ways in our lives to make a way where there seems to be none. I know these things because I have seen them happen with my own eyes. I have received healing. I have watched seemingly bad situations, with no way out, dissolve before my eyes. I have seen and done things, through Christ, that cannot be explained. And I have also been in situations that defied logic in horrible ways. I have been hurt, experienced profound loss, and had other experiences that can make a person question God. In spite of all of it, I still have every reason to believe in God and not a single reason to doubt.

It is because of this that I believe. My beliefs are a part of who I am. They are the filter for most of what I say and do. They create a buffer between me and everyone around me. That buffer creates a lens that allows me to see others the way God might see them. This does not make me perfect. It just makes me cautious. I constantly review what I say and do and compare it to God's mirror. I am constantly asking the questions, "Do my life, words, and actions bring glory to God? Can those around me see God's work in me? Even more, can they see God working through me?" The answer has to be yes.

"Why does the answer have to be yes?" you might ask. Because if I am to act and speak the way I believe, I must, in all things and above all else, look and act like what I believe or I am fake. Others can smell a fake from a mile away. Hard to believe, I know. With all the impossibly crazy things going on in the world right now, we might look at those things and ask, "Are people blind? Have they lost their minds?" But the answer is most likely no. While some may actually be a bit on the crazy side, the reason they believe so emphatically in the things they have been presented with is that they are so disappointed in the options they have been given so far. Christians in church have grown more concerned with their own lives than the lives of the new believer. From my own personal experience, I grew so cold to what others were going through because the Christianity I grew up with seemed superficial. Lord knows I had a plethora of my own problems to deal with.

Please don't misunderstand. I am not saying that all Christians are fake. What I am saying is that in order to be Christians the way we were called to be, we have to ask ourselves if we are Christ-like. Will you proclaim your belief in Jesus Christ if you are in a room full of people who would hurt you if they knew? Not stand up and yell it, but if they asked something like, "Would any who believe in Jesus stand up?" Would you stand up? If you knew you could go to jail or die because of your belief in any given scenario, would you admit to your belief? If the answer is no, then you really don't believe.

I had a really hard time with this question. My spirit wants to immediately say yes. My flesh wants to try and negotiate. The hardest part of this question, if you have never actually been in this situation, is that you really don't know what you would say. That feeling you have inside right now, that doubt in the back of your mind about what you may or may not say, gives you a partial understanding of what Peter was going through after they arrested Jesus and people came and asked him if he knew Jesus.

The key to belief is knowing exactly what you are willing to stand up for. Standing for it when asked to and getting out of the way when you are not. Creating a unity among other believers. Showing them what you believe instead of telling them. Proving what you say with your actions. Living your belief in front of everyone, whether they go to church or not. When a person sees you, they should see your belief. When they hear you, they should know there is something different about you. You should be authentic, intentional, and consistent. If you are not, you risk causing a division in the body of Christ. The truth is if you believe what is written in God's Word, it will flow from you as you live it. What fills your heart will come out in your words and actions.

> *For out of the abundance of the heart his mouth speaks.*
> **Luke 6:45 (NKJV)**

What fills your heart?

The key is to come to terms with who you perceive yourself to be, turn that perception over to God, and open your heart. Ask God to show you who He thinks you are. Ask Him how He sees you. Forgive the person you were, and receive the gift of new life that God reveals to you. If in your heart, you truly have decided to believe, then you will hear what God has to say about you. He will pour into you the thoughts of who you were called to be. It's up to you to receive it. Will you?

Foundations of Faith

The thing about God's gift of faith is that you cannot do anything to build it, grow it, or earn it. No action you perform is going to give you faith, save one. That one thing is to decide with all of your being that you believe that God is. Sounds simple. It is.

Whether it is out loud in a church service, simply raising your hand when asked, or in prayer between you and God, upon confession of your belief in God, He (the creator of all things) comes to you. That's right, He comes to you. Hearing your confession of belief, He comes to you, not because of anything you have done, but because you are still not righteous enough to survive being in the presence of God.

The creator of all things hears your confession, stops what He is doing, and hand delivers the gift of faith that is literally the only requirement for you to be made righteous enough to enter His presence. The keys to His kingdom are provided by the King Himself. We each get a different amount of faith, but the amount you are given is exactly the amount you need to perform the task God has called you to. Will you be a good steward of that gift?

If you are, God is faithful to bring you more. Like the Israelites in the desert receiving manna from heaven, He gives us exactly the amount we need for the task before us. If we are not greedy, and if we use it the way He intends, He gives us more.

As you grow in your relationship with God, He will take you to and through things that require varying degrees of faith. He is always faithful to provide, and He will always walk with you through it. The question is: What will you do with your gift of faith? Use it or lose it? Stand on your firm foundation of faith from your belief that you have placed in God, and stand. Whatever may come, stand. Stand so that others may see God's love. Stand so that others may know God's heart. Stand so that the darkness sees the light and hides. Stand because He who is in you is greater than he who is in the world (**see 1 John 4:1-6**).

Love God

Once God's gift of faith is coursing through your veins, and you eat, breathe, and dream about God's Word, a bond forms. A bond between you and God that—if you feed it with His Word, His will, and His faith—you will see blossom into a powerful thing. When you invite God into your life and really open up to Him, He begins to clean the house, the house of your heart.

The thing about God is that He doesn't want you only on the weekend or Wednesday nights. He doesn't just want you when you feel up to it or only when you're scheduled to serve at church. He wants all of you or nothing.

In life, how would you feel if someone handed you half a pen to sign a contract? Half a hammer to build a house? Half a wrench to repair a car? What if someone gave you a car with no wheels to get to work in? God does not want to rob you of the blessing He has for you if you accept only part of what you need to receive it. He wants total commitment. If you can give Him all of you, He is faithful to give you all of Him. When that happens, every blessing will come to you, shaken together, pressed down into your life, and overflowing into the lives of those around you (**see Luke 6:38**).

A relationship with God is just like a relationship with any other person you may care about. It requires commitment, communication, time, and understanding. A relationship with God will consume you like a fire, but you will be made new every step of the way. Like a forest burned with fire, the beauty that will grow in place of your old self will be evident to all who knew you. The work that God has done in your life will be the encouragement and the fuel for the fire of change that begins in the lives of those around you.

Like mine, your past may have been riddled with pain, shame, and regret. However, a relationship with God turns every minute of your story into a testimony of triumph for those around you. That painful memory in your past becomes the reason someone you may meet finds the strength to keep going. That shame from your past becomes the hope for forgiveness for someone just like you. With God in your heart in abundance, that is what others see pouring out of you, and they want that too. Why?

Why not?

Love the New You

As your relationship with God grows, the image of who you are to Him begins to come into view. This image of who you are called to be is still a choice you have to make. Do you want to be the same old you? Or would you like to experience a new adventure with God leading the way? After all, you did turn to Him for help.

God sees all and knows all. He knew you before you were born, He knew when you would decide to follow Him, and He knows what you're going to choose next. His joy comes from your choice to allow Him into your life. To lead you. To teach you. To break you.

Breaking doesn't sound like a good thing, but I promise you it is. More of Him and less of you. The more we allow God to break us, the more we begin to hear His voice and operate in His will. God knows your heart already. When we allow Him to break us, He begins to show us His heart. His heart shows us how to love and be loved, how to give and to be open to receive. God is love. The more you let Him break you, the closer you get to looking like Christ. As this transformation happens, you begin to move when God says move. You begin to give with a cheerful heart. The best part is that you learn to forgive completely. Starting with you.

You may never have thought about forgiving yourself. I know I didn't. I assumed that because God forgave me, all was done. But I was wrong. I was constantly being pulled back into my past for things I had done. Sins committed both with and against others. Thoughts I had entertained. Secrets that no one knew. God knew, and so did I. Naturally, the devil uses what we are trying to keep hidden in his darkness against us. That simple fact is exactly why God's light and heart are so important to our new selves. Remember, the darkness cannot hide in the light.

I have come to view darkness as the devil's own storage closet. The problem is that when we try to hide our sins, we are actually putting them in the devil's closet and expecting him not to peek. Like that's going to happen. The biggest liar in the universe has not only provided the storage for your dark past, but he has also kept a key for himself. Why? For the simple fact that he has so little power over you that he has to steal from you in order to use your past against you. The plain truth is if we are willing to tell God all of our sins, shames, and wrongs, He is faithful to take them and give us peace and forgiveness in return. Completely.

This simple transaction with God, when done willingly and with a penitent heart, will take away all guilt and shame for the actions and words of our old self. Consequences of our actions and words are still ours to own, but God is faithful to provide healing in those areas too. To be clear, God will forgive you for murder just as quickly as He will lying. Why? Because in God's eyes, the two sins have equal weight, as do all sins except one: blasphemy against His Spirit (**see James 2:10-11; Matthew 12:31**).

Even though God forgives and removes the shame and guilt of our sins, it does not mean that this world will. Shattered trust and the pain of loss will follow us when it comes to the world around us. Why? Remember how the devil uses the things we hide in his darkness against us. It works for those we've wronged as well. When we sin against others (i.e. murder, adultery, lying, stealing), we inevitably create sin in their lives as well. Unforgiveness, hate, offense, and other negatives can all be created in others by the actions and words we allow into the world through us.

When we come to God, those things are forgiven inside of us. For others, these things linger. It is up to us to make amends. Up to us to ask for forgiveness as God leads. I say as God leads because it may not be prudent to immediately go to someone you have sinned against and ask forgiveness. God has a plan, and if you are truly allowing Him to lead, you will wait for His leading before moving on these emotionally charged longings.

In my life, I wait for God's grace. For me, this feels like a joy deep inside my soul that often conflicts with what my head is saying. As an example, there was a person I had conflict with. If I had simply gone to that person at the moment I felt it necessary, they may not have been ready to receive my apology. Then my premature action would have made the situation worse and even created more sin in that person's life by offending them. Because I waited until I felt that release in my soul, I was able to apologize at just the right moment that created joy and peace instead of offense.

I say all of this to paint a picture of the process of getting to know the new you, forgiving the old you, and in turn, loving the new you so completely that your opinion of the new you is that of a child in the embrace of a loving and wise grandparent, parent, or friend. Someone who you know so well that your heart leaps for joy at the sound of their name. That kind of love for yourself is what I like to imagine God's love for us is, with one giant addition: no conditions. God will continue to love you even if you mess up. None of us are perfect. We all mess up, sometimes daily. God knows this. He expects it. Each and every time you mess up, lay it down completely at His feet and ask for forgiveness. Believe with everything that you are that God desires to grant that forgiveness, and embrace that love for you from Him. Then, give it back.

Love Others

Loving others is easier once you have mastered the steps listed previously. Believe that God is and that He desires to have a meaningful relationship with you, that He wants to give you purpose and identity in Himself. Let God then meet you and accept the gift of faith that He brings so you may be made righteous through it and be granted access to His holy presence. With that access, spend time with Him, grow with Him, and learn from Him. Let Him develop the image of the new you that He sees and take on that new identity freely. Love Him with everything you are. Walk daily with Him. While doing so, learn to forgive your old self so that you might love the new you without question and without condition, just as Christ loved the church.

This all done, take that love that now rests in your heart and give it away freely to others. Give of your time, finances, and belongings to those who truly need it. Let them see what God has done in your life. Run toward the affliction of others and help them fight it. Let them know of every detail of your past and what God did to set you free. Let your shame and pain be a testimony of strength to those who still struggle. Be who God has called you to be.

A story that touches my heart, and still inspires me to be better at this, is one of the selfless actions of a friend of mine. The story goes that one night he was driving down the street and he saw a woman lying in the middle of the sidewalk. He stopped to see what was going on, and upon walking up to the woman, he soon realized that she was pregnant. A short conversation with her revealed that she had no place to stay and nothing to eat.

My friend, who we will call Brian, had another person in the car with him at the time and decided to do something about this. Brian and his copilot invited the woman into the car and drove her to a nearby hotel. They paid for her to stay and informed the front desk that she could stay as many nights as she needed and gave the hotel a card for the charges. They bought her a meal and spent a few minutes sharing God and His love with her before leaving. They told her where they go to church and that if she felt like it, she should come and visit. That next Sunday, guess who was in church? That young woman would become a member of that church and go on to do some great things in the community and in the lives of other women with similar stories.

Sharing your testimony with someone else is probably the single most powerful tool you have short of God's Holy Spirit. Lives change when the person living them realizes that things can change. Remember when you were still dealing with your old life? Remember how things looked so bleak? The storm was just too powerful. The wind was too strong. The waves were just too tall. But God ...

If we are to truly be Christ-like, we need to be willing to go out into someone else's storm and stand on the water to show them what is possible if they believe. God's love shines so brightly from us that we literally become lighthouses in their storms. Then if they just don't think they can make it, we reach down below the waters of their storm and pull them up to stand with us. We walk with them in our churches, communities, and families across the top of their storm. We walk with them and pray with them. Asking God's will and miraculous intervention in their lives, we ask God to forgive them. We show them what it looks like to forgive those who have done them wrong. We show them how to walk with God. We show them how to love, how to pray, how to study, and how to live.

Almost everyone knows when they have done wrong. They don't need more judges reminding them and passing judgment on them. They don't need someone reinforcing the condemnation they already feel. They don't need anyone to shine a light on their shame and bring unwanted attention to it. They need someone to forgive them. They need someone to love them. They need someone to just be there for them. They need someone like you.

The Call

If you feel like God is calling you to be that someone for another person, pay attention to His call. He longs for a relationship with you, and the purpose and identity He has for you is yours. It's free. And it's only for you.

When you decide in your heart and mind that God is, and that His promises are real, the only thing you need to do is believe it. Then make up your mind that the relationship with Him that He is calling you to is worth changing your lifestyle, habits, and mannerisms for. When everything in you says, "God, here I am! Use me!" Then you are ready for God to bring you that gift of faith. Repent. As your first act in this new relationship, ask God to forgive you of your sins. Ask Him to teach you what to do and how to be. Ask Him to break you so that there is no part of you that is hidden from Him.

Find a church body where they teach you to grow in Him, where they walk alongside you, and provide strength in your weakness, where you can find encouragement when you feel doubt and shelter when the storms of your life feel like they are too much. Be baptized so that your flesh and spirit may both be cleansed of the sins of your past. Let God's Holy Spirit fill every area of your mind, heart, and soul. Let His will be the focus of your every day. Let Him make you righteous with His gift of faith, and then walk in it with Him. Find your path next to Him and flow in His grace.

When you find that place, stay there as long as God stays with you. Follow Him. He may lead you elsewhere, and that's ok. He may have something more for you. He may need you to grow. The plan He has for you may require an experience that you need to have. Like mine, some of your experiences may be painful. But if you walk with Him, He is faithful to protect and guide you. He will give you grace to walk through those fires, and He will send help to keep you in the midst of them. God is good, and His mercy endures.

Be bold and courageous in the Lord. Let your faith shine bright. Your past will be washed away, along with the shame and guilt. The enemy will try and remind you of your past. He will try and use it against you. His goal is to put just enough in your path to get you to sin again. No one is perfect, and you will make mistakes. That's ok. God is still there.

He will never leave you or forsake you. God is the same, always (**see Hebrews 13:5-8**). All you have to do is turn back to Him and ask for forgiveness and believe He will.

Whether the circumstances of your life are good or bad, rich or poor; whether you find yourself sick or well, in all things, give thanks to God. This flesh we live in is temporary. God made it; He can heal it. We live according to His kingdom, so finances come from Him. Give thanks and be happy, no matter your circumstances. This is part of faith. No evil thing comes from God. So be strong, and believe!

EPHESIANS 6:13 (NLT)

Therefore, put on every piece of God's armor so you will be able to resist the enemy in the time of evil. Then after the battle you will still be standing firm.

www.ingramcontent.com/pod-product-compliance
Lightning Source LLC
Chambersburg PA
CBHW071246070526
44583CB00017B/2342